Say What?

Colloquialisms

A look back at colloquialisms and other witty sayings from a
by-gone era as recalled by one who's "been there and done that!"

Fred G. Wilson

Outskirts Press, Inc.
Denver, Colorado

Outskirts Press, Inc.
http://www.outskirtspress.com

ISBN: 978-1-4327-2792-5

Library of Congress Control Number: 2008935867

Outskirts Press and the "OP" logo are trademarks belonging to Outskirts Press, Inc.

PRINTED IN THE UNITED STATES OF AMERICA

Table of Contents

About the Author

I have had an interesting and busy life since coming into this world in 1935. After high school, I spent four years in the U.S. Navy, spending two years in the Far East.

Upon separation from active duty, I married and moved to Orlando, Florida, and enrolled in college. Due to a severe head injury to our son, Gary, it was necessary to return to our home state of Kentucky so he could receive treatment until he recovered. In December, 1964, the family moved back to Florida to Cocoa Beach and Merritt Island. I was employed for about five years at Kennedy Space Center from Gemini 7 through Apollo 11. Two major events that occurred while there were the fire and subsequent death of the three astronauts training for Apollo 1, and later the moon landing of Apollo 11. Astronauts Neil Armstrong and Buzz Aldrin landed on the moon's surface, while Michael Collins remained aboard the Command Module awaiting their return.

In 1970 the family moved to Arlington, Texas, so I could attend Bible Baptist Seminary. I graduated in May, 1973, with a Bachelor of Divinity degree.

Since then, I have served as pastor or interim pastor in Idaho, Tennessee, Colorado, Florida and Kentucky. From 1979 through 1999, I was bi-vocational, being employed as a letter carrier with the U.S. Postal Service while also serving in the gospel ministry. I retired from the last pastorate in April, 1997, and retired from the U.S. Postal Service in December, 1999. I was employed as a full-time teacher for four years at a private Christian school and as a substitute teacher for two years from 2000 through 2007.

I am well acquainted with personal tragedy and grief. My oldest daughter, Donna, passed away on August 3, 2002, at the age of 39 after a lengthy battle with cancer. My wife, Janet, passed away on February 9, 2006, at the age of 58 of heart failure. My oldest son, Gary, passed away on March 11, 2006, at the age of 47 after succumbing to lymphoma cancer. Prior to that, Gary had suffered total kidney failure and had received a donor kidney as a transplant. He was unable to regain his former physical abilities that would allow him to be regularly employed.

Presently, I am living in Tennessee with my new wife, Linda, whom I met through eHarmony.com. She is a wonderful lady and I am thankful for her.

Therefore, the humor, proverbs, tall tales, and other assorted "gems" are helpful to me as I cope with life's ups and downs. It is my sincere wish that they will "tickle your fancy" and bring a chuckle or two as you absorb them.

My Mom's Dad, Grandpa Jesse Benton, had a profound influence upon my life. He was one of the "neatest" persons I have ever known and I loved him dearly. Needless to say, I learned a great deal from observing and listening to him as a youngster. Enjoy!

Fred G. Wilson, Author

Preface

Having been born during the Depression in 1935, I was raised during some very trying times in our nation's history. We as a nation were thrust onto the world's stage with the onset of World War 2 and, thus, began to come out of the doldrums as a result.

It was against this backdrop of events that I had my early childhood memories and the experiences that forged me into the adult that I became. During this period, times were hard and folks learned to get by with what they had and were generally thankful for the things that they did have.

Having a sense of humor seemed to ease the misery of those by-gone days, and people poked fun at each other and sought to make light of the woes they were experiencing. Out of this era came some colorful, humorous and enlightened sayings. In every part of our nation there were colloquial expressions that summed up the feelings of the local region. This book contains some of these from the Southeast region, and is by no means an all-inclusive summary. Perhaps every reader who peruses these pages will recall some that are not included herein.

Many of these expressions were learned at home from Mom and Dad. This was before television and we learned to amuse ourselves with "home-grown" entertainment. Farm work, taking care of the livestock, and the many chores kept us busy. When I reflect back on those days, I wouldn't change them even if I could.

I wish to dedicate this book to Mom and Dad, who "Being dead, yet speaketh." My Dad's name was Cornelius (Neal) Wilson, Sr. (b.

1887, d. 1970), and my Mom's name was Amanda Kathryn Benton Wilson (b. 1893, d. 1977.) They brought ten children into this world and successfully raised them all. Quite an accomplishment!

The origin of many of these sayings is obscure to me. When I was a youngster hearing them, they were just a normal part of our everyday conversations. People talked to each other more then than they do now. Modern communication technology and the fast-paced life style today precludes the intimacy of yesteryear. In many ways, we have lost something very special with our helter-skelter way of life today.

It is because "the times, they are changing", that I undertook to recall some of the memories of my youth. This is a different world today when compared to when I was a boy. I want to preserve for my children, their children, and future generations those events and expressions that I grew up with. Those by-gone days contain many precious memories for me.

Recalling these gems has truly been a pilgrimage of pure joy. As I reflect upon these sayings, I remember when and where I heard them and how some of them came into being. It is my wish that you will find enjoyment with them.

Fred G. Wilson, Author

The Cornelius ("Neal") Wilson family. From left to right:
Front row: Fred; Second row: Glenn, Cornelius Jr.; Virgil
and Mary; Third row: Mom, Glydus ("Tootsie"), Audrey
and Dad; Fourth row: Ruth, Carl and Russell.

The Wilson family farmhouse.

"Neal" Wilson grocery, a.k.a. Wilson's "Jot'em down" store.

Grandpa Jesse James Benton.

Chapter 1

Countrified Humor

F.G.W.
#1

TAKING A BATH IN #2 WASH TUB

D uring my "growing up" years, one constant that seemed to always be present was the usage of humor in our every-day speech. Looking back on it now, I realize that it was probably a built-in mechanism that helped folks to endure and cope with the realities of life in rural America after the Depression and during World War 2. Some of them were real "knee slappers" and would "tickle your funny bone."

For example, if you wanted to convey the fact that someone was busy, you might say that he was "busier than a sack full of cats."

1

Now, can you imagine what's going on inside a sack full of cats? They would be busy, let me assure you! Another way of expressing this is, "He's busier than a one-armed paper hanger with an itch!" Or, "Busier than a one-legged man in a butt-kicking contest!"

If someone wasn't doing his share of trying to earn a living, and would "mooch" off of you, you might tell him, "I didn't take you to raise!" Mom used to say, "Lean on your own breakfast", which was another way of saying the same thing.

If someone asked you to do something that you was in favor of, you might say, "I don't 'care' if I do." ("I don't 'mind' if I do!")

When offered a second portion of food that you liked, you might hear, "Have another 'helping' of...." Not a spoon full of; a slice of; a cup of; but a "helping."

Country folks mostly were honest, hard-working people who lived by the Golden Rule. They just wanted a fair chance at life and wanted a "level playing field." Sometimes things didn't go well and you could hear certain expressions that conveyed their lack of pleasure at that moment, such as, "dag nab it," "darn it," "dog gone it," "gosh dog amighty," etc. My favorite one of all is: "dirty, rats-a-frattin', cotton-pickin', dad jimmed, flag donged, rinky dink, skiddle-dee wonkus, sass-a-frassin', mangy low-down good for nothing scum ball!" God-fearing and church-going folks just didn't cuss. So, they "took the edge off" by watering down their language.

When someone couldn't make up his mind about something, he was said to "hem haw." If someone was lazy, he "wouldn't hit a lick at a snake."

If someone wasn't too bright, he was said to be "dumber than a door nail." If something was really dead, it was "deader than a door nail."

To be unstable, you was "crazier than the man in the moon." ("Doesn't know any more than the man in the moon!")

Mom used to have an expression when startled or awed. She's say, "Well, 'pon my word and honor." It was a while before I figured out that "'pon" was a short version of "upon". She also would say, "Well, as I live and breathe!"

One that really says it all is, "He's got ants in his pants." This means he was restless.

If something was going to happen quickly, it was said to happen in "three shakes of a lamb's tail." If you've ever watched a lamb when its sucking its mother's milk, you will see its tail shaking back and forth faster than the blink of an eye!

When someone was disagreeable, he was said to be as "ill as a copperhead." To fully appreciate this remark, you need to understand that a copperhead is a poisonous snake that is noted for striking from ambush, and is not afraid of humans. They are "short-tempered" and will strike you if you "crowd" them. Another expression that's not very complimentary is to tell someone he is "lower than a snake's belly." That's not very nice!

Someone who doesn't go along "with the crowd" is said to be "as independent as a hog on ice."

If someone wasn't considered to be big enough to be a threat, he was said to be "too small to whip a cat."

To be "happy as a lark" meant you was "tickled pink." Or, if you was "grinning like a 'possum" you was really elated.

When someone was "antsy" about something, he was "more nervous than a cat in a room full of rocking chairs!"

How about "naked as a jay bird?" How naked is that? Or, if you hadn't seen someone in quite a while, you hadn't seen him "in a coon's age" or "in a month of Sundays."

To be in a position where you had to make a difficult decision, and either way it was going to be tough, you was "between a rock and a hard place!"

In our English language, the words "if" and "but" make a world of difference. Therefore, "if 'ifs' and 'buts' were candy and nuts, we'd all have a merry Christmas."

When you was very warm, you was "hotter than a cat on a tin roof in the middle of August," or "hotter than blue blazes." On the other hand, if you was unfeeling, you was said to be "colder than an old maid's heart!"

Something that was plentiful was said to be "as common as ten-penny nails."

If someone wasn't much of a fighter, it was said that "he couldn't fight his way out of a wet paper sack."

This one I know from personal experience growing up on the farm. We took a bath every Saturday, whether we needed it or not! (Where's that # 2 wash tub?) My brother, Glenn, related to me how we were told to bathe when we were taking a bath in the # 2 wash tub. We were to wash down as far as "possible." Then, we were to wash up as far as "possible." Then, we were to wash "possible!" Isn't that a hoot? Country humor!

To express the fact that you wasn't going to wait for someone else, you was said to be "waiting like one hog waits on another!" (To fully appreciate this, you have to understand that hogs are not noted for waiting for other hogs when it's feeding time!)

If something was hard, it was "harder than a pine knot." To be really tough, you was "tougher than 'whang' leather." Does anyone know what "whang" leather is?

Also, "birds of a feather tend to flock together." This means that people seem to seek out other people like themselves.

If something wasn't funny, you might hear: "That's about as funny as a skunk in church."

How about, "If I go any faster, I'm going to get ahead of myself?" Would you run that one by me one more time?

If something was tangled, it was said to be a "granny knot."

When the first freeze came, usually around Thanksgiving Day, my Dad would get two or three men in the neighborhood to help him kill and butcher hogs. This was an all-day job and it was usually well into the night before it was completed. Nothing was wasted from the hogs. Mostly, things like the head, feet, and other not-so-desirable parts were given to anyone who wanted them. To drive home the point about using all of the hogs, it was said that "the only thing not consumed was the squeal!"

If someone was good natured, he was said to "have a heart of gold, and teeth to match." How about "If I was any happier, I'd be ashamed?"

When someone butted in where he wasn't wanted, you might hear, "Who pulled your chain?" (This goes back to the days of bare ceiling lights with a pull chain to turn the light on and off.)

When my son, Gary, was living with a kidney transplant, sometimes he wouldn't be feeling very well, and he'd be irritable. On one occasion three of my children and their spouses, and a house full of grandkids were visiting at my home. The grandkids were noisy and running around and they got on Gary's nerves. He told the kids to "quiet down." My son, Wayne, casually said to Gary, "Who made you the hall monitor?" That "broke the ice" and things were ok then.

When someone wasn't very fast at something, you might hear this one: "Grandma was slow, but she had an excuse. She was old!" Another way of saying this was to be told, "You're slower than molasses in January!"

If you want to know what cold weather is really like, this quote says it all: "It's colder than a well digger's backside in January!"

If you was nearly broke (no money), you "didn't have two nickels to rub together." Or, you was "as poor as Job's turkey." If something was of little value, it was said to be "about as useless as a side saddle on a hog."

My Dad used to tell us boys this zinger: "It's easy, if you know how!" Duh!

Another way of saying you wasn't lazy was to say that you "was as busy as a cat clawing at a hornet's nest." Can't you just see that cat fighting off about a zillion hornets that are trying to sting him?

Say, what's worse than finding a worm in your apple? Half a worm, of course! I guess about the worse thing that can happen to a school-age kid is for him to go to school and the parents move away before he returns home!

Have you ever been thirsty? How about: "I'm so thirsty I'm spitting up cotton?" When you can't figure something out, you say "I can't make heads or tails of it."

I remember Mom admonishing us boys, "Don't forget to wash behind your ears." When leaving the house to go somewhere, she'd tell us: "Don't forget your manners."

When we were told to do something by our Dad, if we said "wait", he'd tell us, "Wait" (weight) is what broke the bridge down!" If we said "can't" when we were told to do something, Dad would say, "'Can't' never could do anything!"

If something really smelled badly, it was said to "stink worse than rotten eggs." Folks, if you've never smelled rotten eggs, you've missed a lulu. Whew!

If a child was restless, he was said to "wiggle like a bowl full of Jell-O." Remember this jewel: "Two wrongs don't make a right?"

Did you know that "a bird in hand is worth two in the bush?" Mom used to say: "Once an adult, twice a child. (You need help at the beginning and at the end of your lifetime.)

One valuable lesson I learned while a youngster concerned when we were going somewhere in Dad's car. He chewed tobacco all of his adult life, and when traveling he would need to spit tobacco juice out the window from time to time. It didn't take me long to realize that sitting behind him on the back seat was not the place to be. I can tell you from personal experience that tobacco juice really stings when it gets in your eyes!

If you couldn't figure something out, you was said to be "stumped" or "up a tree." If you didn't know where you was, you was "as lost as a goose in a hail storm."

If something was unlawful, it was said to be "as crooked as a sack full of elbows," or "as crooked as a dog's hind leg." or "as crooked as a barrel of fish hooks."

If you was in favor of something, you was "fur" it. If you was against something, you was "agin" it.

I can remember as a youngster when products associated with famous cartoon characters were offered for sale to kids who followed the cartoon characters' antics. Every kid wanted to own the products offered for sale, such as a lunch box, article of clothing, comic books, coloring books, toys, etc.

If you was leery of something, you was said to be "like a calf looking at a new gate." (Ask any cattle raiser, and he can explain that one to you.)

In the '40s and '50s, there were still a lot of men who wore a pocket watch to keep the time. If you had a "railroad pocket watch", you had a good one. Companies that made wrist watches tended to be rather expensive until other companies began to manufacture wrist watches that were relatively inexpensive and more folks could afford them. After that, wrist watches came into vogue. I have owned several of them over the years, and have been quite satisfied with their reliability.

If you refused to work, you was said to "balk, like a mule." If you was a poor shot with a gun, you couldn't "hit the side of a barn with a bass fiddle!" To be really lazy, you was "lazier than a hound dog lying on a thorn."

A not too gracious way of saying something was slick was to say it was "slicker than snot on a glass door knob." Or, "slicker than a greased pig." I remember at the county fair years ago one of the attractions was you had to grab hold of and maintain your grip on a pig that was greased. Another version of this was to grease a wooden pole and you had to try to climb it. Not likely!! If you was fast, you was said to be as "fast as greased lightning!" Now, that's fast! If you was "antsy", you was "as nervous as a Mexican jumping bean."

When you didn't think something was funny, you might say, "That's about as funny as a bucket full of hiccups."

When someone had the ability to make money easily, he was said to be making money "hand over fist." If something was fast, it was as "quick as a wink."

One admonition I heard often as I was growing up was to "hurry up every chance you get!" When folks were leaving after having visited us, you was sure to hear Mom say: "Take your time going, but hurry back."

.When Mom was amazed about something, she might say: "Well, bless my buttons," or, "Well, bless my soul." My sister, Ruth, would express it this way: "Well, bless old Miss Agnes." Ruth also used to say, "Shake up your muddy water" when you was trying to remember something.

When trying to trade or swap for something, and you wanted to "call their bluff", you might say, "There it is, take it or leave it." If something wasn't of much value, it was said that it "didn't amount to a hill of beans."

When you got a good rain, you might hear it described as a "gully washer" or a "frog choker." If it was raining really hard, it was said to be "raining cats and dogs!"

Someone who couldn't sing very well was said to be "unable to carry a tune in a bucket." Or, "If you're singing that song in parts, leave my part out."

When you arose early in the morning, you was said to "get up before breakfast." If you went to bed late at night, and arose early the next morning, you "got in one side of the bed and slid out the other!"

When someone passed away and folks didn't think the deceased had much prospect of going to heaven, he was "all dressed up and nowhere to go!"

Mom used to admonish us kids to "eat something that will stick to your ribs." Or, when sitting at the dining table we were urged to "tank up!" If we didn't eat much, we were told "you didn't eat enough to keep a canary alive!"

When someone needed to correct their behavior, he was admonished to "straighten up and fly right."

Country folks have a vocabulary of their own. They are especially noted for omitting the letter "g" on their verbs ending in "ing". Examples of this are: "fishin', huntin', swimmin', sleepin'," etc.

From my earliest childhood I recall being told by my parents to answer "No, Sir", "Yes, Sir", "No, Ma'am", "Yes, Ma'am" to our elders. That's a rarity now-a-days.

Sometimes Dad would get weary of hearing us boys use the word "if" in our conversation. To get our attention about this, he'd say, "If a frog had wings, he wouldn't have to hop along on his hind end!"

If you thought you was better than anyone else, you might just hear: "Just who do you think you are, _____ _____?" (Some famous person.)

If two people were unlike each other, they were said to be "as different as night and day" or "as different as black and white."

When you was required to do something that was unpleasant, it was said to be "a bitter pill to swallow."

It seemed that I could never get away with anything when I was growing up. I finally came up with the conclusion that Mom and Dad had "eyes in the back of their heads."

If someone was stingy with their money, he was said to be a "tight wad." And, that person was said to still have "the first dollar that he earned." If someone was well off financially, he was said to be "well to do."

When we were asked to try hard to remember something, Mom would tell us to "put on your 'thinking cap'."

When someone was particular or choosey about something, he was said to be "picky-u-nish."

When someone was undertaking something that was difficult, and it was barely accomplished and only after much effort, it was said to have been done "by the skin of his teeth!"

I can remember Mom cautioning us boys to be careful about our appearance when we went anywhere away from home. She would tell us not to leave home "looking like a rag picker." During the Depression and World War 2, it wasn't uncommon for folks who were "down on their luck" to go about gathering rags and other items that could be sold at the junk yard in order to make a little money for necessities of life. So, if we left home and we weren't properly dressed, we might "look like a rag picker." We were farm folks and we never lacked for food or clothing or shelter, but Mom always wanted us to look our best when we were away from home. Mom used to say, "You might have patches on your clothes, but they'll be clean patches!" It was a matter of character to her.

One thing that I can easily recall while growing up on the farm was that we never wasted anything that was useful. Even though we never wanted for food or basic necessities, we were cautioned to never waste things. We never took anything for granted. Mom's way of expressing this truth was by telling us: "Waste not, want not."

When something came up that needed attention, but it was already too late to do anything about it, it was said to be "water under the bridge."

Many rural parents, especially Moms, used to tell their daughters that the way to a man's heart was through his stomach. Thus, daughters were encouraged to learn to be good cooks so they someday might "catch a man" with their culinary abilities. In my sister's, (Tootsie), kitchen there is a plaque that reads: "Kissin' don't last, cookin' do!"

When folks were economically depressed ("dirt poor"), and they tried by "hook or by crook" to elevate themselves to a higher social level, they were said to be "trying to keep up with the Joneses!" Sometimes they tried to improve their social standing by marrying "upward." At times this effort was so obvious that it was almost comical to observe. A familiar expression that addressed this was "don't get above your raising!" One wonderful aspect of living in America is that people are usually limited only by their own willingness to work hard in order to improve their status in life.

Another humorous little "ditty" that I heard often while growing up was an expression that was used when something was really rare or non-existent. In that case, it was said to be "as scarce as hen's teeth!" (Have you ever seen any teeth in a hen's mouth? Me neither!)

If people were doing well economically, and were prosperous, they were said to be "living high on the hog!" On the other hand, if people were living "above their means", they were said to "have a

9

beef steak appetite, but a hamburger pocket book!"

When country folks give directions, it's not the same as city folks. For example, when country folks ask how far it is from point "A" to point "B", they might say that it's about three miles "as the crow flies." Now, every rural resident knows what that means. (It's the same as "the shortest distance between two points is a straight line.") But, the country roads of years ago weren't built in a "straight line." Therefore, the curvy, circuitous rural road distances were calculated as so many "country miles." A country mile is not the same as an interstate mile of today's highways. In other words, if you drove for one mile years ago, you would have actually only gone perhaps one/half mile in actual straight-line distance because of the curves, up and down the hills, etc. But, when you drive on today's modern freeways, a mile traveled is closer to an actual mile in straight-line distance "as the crow flies!"

An expression that I heard a "million" times as I was growing up had to do with someone who was attempting to undertake something that was beyond his capacity to do. Just as sure as "Heaven is up", he would hear someone say, "He can't do that, he's still wet behind his ears!" That meant that he wasn't prepared or capable of undertaking that task. When a baby is born, he is covered with fluids from his mother, and is just starting on the "journey" that is to be his life. Thus, "He's still wet behind his ears!"

It wasn't unusual for parents or older siblings to "stretch the truth" a tad in order to get a youngster to correct his behavior. For example, when a small child was having a "crying jag" because he was either hurt or didn't get his way, his face would surely be contorted "out of shape." When this happened, he would likely be told, "I hope your face doesn't freeze like that!" The reason for being told this, of course, is to try to get the child to "straighten up" and quit crying. I must say that this rarely ever caused the child to stop "being out of sorts." Did you ever wonder why there's no "owner's manual" when you become parents? I guess parenting is an "on-the-job" process. GOOD LUCK!!

One memory that I recall from the years on the farm was when it was time to "slop" the hogs. This was when we took table scraps out to the hogs' feeding troughs and fed them. They would eat just about anything that you gave them. And, it always seemed that no matter what you fed them, they were happy to get it. So, if someone was really thrilled about some turn of events, it was said that he was in "hog heaven!"

And, speaking of hogs, Dad used to say that "even a blind hog will stumble across an acorn ever now and then." A hog likes to root with its nose for things to eat, such as acorns, nuts, etc. They will get under the branches of an oak tree, and try to root out acorns to eat. So, the expression about the blind hog means that even unskilled folks will sometimes get lucky and perform some deed at which they are not proficient.

An incident that occurred when I was about ten years old left a vivid impression on me. One day I was in the bedroom that my brother, Junior, and I shared. I was reading the tag on the end of my pillow that read, "Do not remove tag under penalty of law", or words to that effect. Anyway, the tag came off and Junior really "laid it on thick" about how the "tag patrol" was going to come and get me and haul me off to jail. Well, it scared me something awful.. I could just see myself behind bars for some lengthy period of time. And, it wasn't until Mom had reassured me that I wasn't going to jail that I was able to calm down. Junior liked to tease people a lot.

If you was faced with a difficult task or confronted with something that you found little pleasure in, it was said to be "a hard row to hoe."

When someone was stubborn or "set in his ways", he was said to be "bull headed!" If you was going to meet something "head-on", you was going to "take the bull by the horns!"

Chapter 2

Whoppers, Tall Tales, and Other Outrageous Offerings

BIRD DOG SKELETON ON 'POINT'

F.G.W. #2

Since there was no television when I was growing up on the farm, there was a lot of story-telling to amuse us in our "spare" time. Some of the tales were fascinating and would hold our rapt attention. I eagerly listened to my Mom and Dad, my grandfather Benton, and other elderly folks relate events of their younger days.

Grandpa Benton used to like to tell riddles and we were asked to figure them out. One riddle that I recall that he told us was this one: "Round as a biscuit, busy as a bee, prettiest little thing that you ever did see." We, of course, strained our brains and offered several

13

answers, but they were all wrong. Finally, after struggling with it for a while, he told us the answer. It was a pocket watch!

Grandpa Benton would come spend several weeks at our farm every year, usually in the late fall or winter. I remember one time he came in the winter time. At night he and I would sleep together in the same bed. As usual, Mom had fried potatoes and pinto beans every day and I was bloated with gas and was "about to bust!" That night we went to bed and we had the covers pulled up to our chins because it was really cold. I wanted to pass gas really bad, but I didn't want to let Grandpa Benton know when I did it. Anyway, I couldn't hold it any longer and I "let her rip!" Grandpa Benton said, "Fred, did you toot poot?" I answered, "Yes, Grandpa." He said, "Whew, I thought so!"

Another one that's attributed to Grandpa Benton was really outrageous. I don't know the validity of it, but it was handed down to me by some kinfolks when I was in my teens. The story had to do with sitting up with a corpse back in the early part of the last century. To really appreciate the story, you have to understand that when this was supposed to have happened, folks were laid out in a casket in the front parlor of homes and not so much in a funeral home. It was common practice for someone to sit up with the corpse overnight out of respect for the deceased person. Well, as the story goes, someone in the family had passed away and was laid out in a casket in the parlor of a house. It was in late July and it was really hot. Folks were milling around and the funeral parlor fans were going like "a house on fire." Around ten o'clock in the evening the people began to leave for their own homes. Grandpa Benton said that he would sit up with the corpse overnight and that everyone else could go home.

In those days, men's pants had buttons to close the fly. This was before the wide-spread use of zippers. Anyway, Grandpa Benton's fly was unbuttoned. When Mom came in to tell her Dad "good night", she noticed his fly was unbuttoned. When she informed him of this, he told her: "Where there's a corpse, there has to be an open window!" Remember, there's no air conditioning, it's hot, and the parlor window is wide open. According to the tale, Mom turned three shades of red and told her Dad: "Dad, shame on you!" Knowing my Grandpa, this tale is believable!

There was a fellow in our county during the '40s and '50s who had a reputation of being a teller of tall tales. I wont tell you his name, but he was a great teller of "whoppers" and other "stretching of the truth!" Just about everybody knew him and his reputation for "messing around with the truth." One story that he liked to tell had to do with bird dog hunting. According to him, several men took some bird dogs that were pointers and went hunting. One of the dogs was said to be so good at pointing that when he came upon a covey of birds, he wouldn't come off point until the hunters flushed them out. Well, this one time this particular dog came upon birds and he "went to point." He froze in his pointing stance and didn't move from it. The field where they were hunting had grass, weeds and brush up to about waist high. The hunters lost track of the dog. They called him, but he wouldn't come off point. Finally, they gave up and left and returned home. About two years later, some bird hunters were hunting in the same field and came upon the skeleton of a pointer still in his "on point" stance! Now, folks, that's what I call a "whopper!"

`There's another tale told about this fellow that's humorous. Supposedly, this "teller of tall tales" got weary of hearing folks tell him about his "whoppers", so he decided to take a Greyhound bus to Florida. After a day or so, he arrived at Orlando, Florida, and left the bus terminal and started walking down the street. He came upon two boys who were arguing about something. One of the boys told the other one that he didn't believe what he was being told, and told him, "You're a bigger liar than _____ !"(The name that he heard was, of course, his own!) Upon hearing this, he went back to the bus station, bought a return ticket, and went back home!

When us last four children, all boys, were still kids at home, I'm told that we were digging in the back yard one day. Mom told us to stop digging because she didn't want the yard dug up. Evidently, we ignored her warning and she then proceeded to give each of us a whipping. After this, it was decided that the four of us were just going to run away. So, we proceeded to walk to the back of the farm. Fortunately, common sense kicked in and it was reasoned that running away was not such a good idea after all! I must confess I don't remember this episode, but I'm told that it assuredly happened.

This really happened to me. I'm ashamed to tell it, but I must confess that it's true. My sister, "Tootsie" (Glydus), and her husband,

Carter Lowry Peel, had a son whose name was Jerry Rice Peel. Jerry Rice was nearly five years younger than me. When I was about eleven years old, he came out to our farm to spend a few days with us. It was in the summer and we were out-of-doors playing as young boys do, and having a "good old time." One thing led to another and before you know it we were playing "I dare you" games. If you didn't do whatever you was dared to do, you was considered a sissy. Everything went along fine until he dared me to pee in the cistern. To fully appreciate the magnitude of this dare, you have to understand that this was before city water was available in rural areas. Farmers had a cistern which collected water that ran from the roof into it whenever it rained, and water wasn't to be wasted. To make matters worse for me, he "double dared" me. Well, this was a challenge that couldn't be ignored! Anyway, I proceeded to pee into the cistern and then he ran into the house and told Mom what I had just done! Well, I guess you know what happened next! Mom told Dad and I got the whipping of my life. Dad made me go cut a peach tree limb and he whipped me a "good one!" Then, he had to take a bucket and bail out all the water in the cistern. Next, he poured bleach into it and scrubbed it down good. Then, he had to order a truck load of water hauled and put into the cistern. Needless to say, I've never done that again. Jerry Rice is lucky that I didn't break his neck!

I know this one happened because I was there when it happened. My wife, Linda, and I were at Renfro Valley, Kentucky, one Saturday afternoon about 5:30 and we were going to go to the barn dance there later that evening. We were riding around killing time before the show started when I needed to stop at a rest room to relieve myself. I pulled into a service station and Linda said that she would wait in the car for me. I went inside the station and asked where the men's room was and was shown where it was. There was another man ahead of me waiting outside the door. In a few minutes, a man came out of the rest room and the fellow ahead of me went in and closed the door. After a couple of minutes he opened the door and told me I could come on in if I wanted to use the stall where the commode was. I proceeded to do so and while sitting there I decided to call Linda on my cell phone. She had her cell phone also with her in her purse. Now get the picture: I'm in the stall, sitting, and the other fellow is using the urinal on the other side of the stall wall from me. I dialed Linda's cell number and when she answered me, I said, "Are you lonesome out there?" (Out in the car!) Before you can say "Jackie Robinson" this fellow says, "No, not really!" The next thing I hear is the door being quickly opened and closed. He's "cutting a trail" out of there! I guess the poor guy thought I was "hitting up on him." When I went back to the car after I had finished using the rest room, Linda asked me what the fellow's hurry was because he came out of the station, got into his car, and left quickly. When I explained it to her, we both liked to have "busted a gut" from laughing so hard. That was funny!!!

Say, do you know what's round on both ends and "high" in the middle? If you don't figure it out, you're going to feel silly! It's "as plain as the nose on your face!" Give up? The answer is "Ohio!" What has four "eyes" and can't see? It's M"i" ss "i" ss "i" pp"i". (" eyes"="i's"in Mississippi.) Got ya!

As a general rule, children tend to pretty much pattern their lives after their parents. Country folks have an expression that conveys this fact: "An acorn doesn't fall far from the tree."

When someone didn't want to face up to something, or didn't get "to the point", he was said to be "beating around the bush!"

Someone who was clumsy or not very graceful was said to be "like a bull in a china shop!"

Anyone who believed everything that was being said about something was said to swallow it "hook, line and sinker!"

If someone was really stingy with his money, he was said to be "as tight as the bark on a China berry tree!" (I have no idea what a "China berry tree" is!)

Someone who works diligently at a task is said to have "his nose to the grindstone", or "his shoulder to the wheel!"

When you are teasing someone, or telling a "big'un", you are said to be "pulling his leg!"

If you had a bit of bad luck or something unpleasant happened, you was said to "need that like you need a hole in the head!"

To be really familiar with something is to "know it like the back of your hand", or "like the palm of your hand!"

Chapter 3

World War 2

WORLD WAR 2 G.I.

F.G.W.
3

I was in the first grade at the Logana Elementary School in Jessamine County, Kentucky, when World War 2 started with the bombing of Pearl Harbor, Hawaii, by Japan. The four years that followed were trying times, and the entire country pulled together to bring the war to a successful conclusion.

Gasoline, rubber, sugar, metal and other materials needed for the war effort were rationed. There were scrap metal drives, rag drives, savings bonds drives and other means used to aid the cause. My father raised crops under contract with the government to help supply items needed by the military. He raised hemp for making ropes for the U.S. Navy and tomatoes for K-rations for the service men.

Farmers had to be thrifty in the usage of their gasoline rations and used their gasoline-powered equipment sparingly. I remember one fellow who had an older car that had a leaky radiator, and burned motor oil. He would drive up to my Dad's store next to the gas pump and jokingly say, "Gas, oil and water. One gallon of each!"

Since tires were rationed, people learned how to get every mile out of them. One popular item used extensively during those days was a tire boot. A tire boot was a large patch that was placed between the inner tube and the inside of the tire. This was, of course, before the days of tubeless tires. When the tires became slick (bald), the inner tube was more likely to be penetrated and thus lose its air. When this happened, the inner tube was repaired, the boot was placed inside the tire at the place where the tire was punctured, and the tire was remounted on the wheel. Then, the tire was pumped up to the proper air pressure and remounted, and you proceeded on your way. Every time the tire rolled over and passed the boot section, you would get a nice little bump in your ride! You didn't dare leave home without a tire tube repair kit, a tire pump, and tire tools to remove the inner tube for repairs.

There is one incident that stands out in my memory concerning World War 2. One Saturday during the summer of 1943, when I was eight years old, our family went to town to shop as was our custom. After shopping my Dad would go to the front of the courthouse and visit with other farmers, etc. You have to understand that this was a scary time. We were losing soldiers, sailors and airmen at an alarming rate. We weren't sure at this time who would win the war. We were fighting Germany, Italy, Japan, Spain and some smaller countries who had banded together against us. They were known as the Axis nations. As I listened to my Dad and another man talking about the war, and the dire reports that were forthcoming each day, I was afraid. I remember I moved over next to my Dad so I could be close to him. He put his right arm around my shoulder and pulled me close to him. Even though I was afraid, when he did that I knew that I was safe from harm. I knew that my Dad would protect me at all cost. I've never forgotten that!

My brother, Russell, enlisted in the U.S. Army in 1937 for two years because there wasn't any employment opportunities around home. He completed that term and re-enlisted for two more years. This second tour was almost over when World War 2 began. He was obliged to stay in the Army until the war was over in 1945. He served in North Africa, Sicily and Italy during the war as a medical corpsman. I remember when he came home after the war and everyone at home was making a big fuss over him. I asked Mom, "Who's that?" She answered, "Your brother, Russell!" I hadn't seen him for so long that I didn't remember him.

My brother-in-law, Lucian Walker, served in the U.S. Navy as a cook aboard a destroyer in the Pacific theater. His wife, Ruth (my oldest sister), worked in a parachute factory in Lexington, Kentucky. Everyone did their part and helped any way they could.

My oldest brother, Carl, tried repeatedly during World War 2 to enlist into military service, but was unable to pass the physical exam due to heart problems. (It's interesting that when he came to the end of his life on earth, he died of a heart attack.) He went from one service branch to another seeking to enlist, but to no avail. I've heard my parents tell that Carl cried when he wasn't accepted as a result of his health. He wanted so badly to serve his country in the service. As it was, Mom and Dad had five of their six sons to serve honorably in America's armed forces in World War 2 or the Korean War.

In my father's grocery store during the war there was a board with the names of the local service men who were serving in the military. Their names were in blue letters. If one of them was killed in action, his name was replaced with gold letters. In the homes of the service men there would be a blue star placed in the front window to testify that someone in that family was serving in the military service. If any were killed in action, the blue star would be replaced by a gold one.

By the grace of God the Allies won the victory and our way of life was preserved.

Chapter 4

Braggadocio and Bravado

PUT UP YOUR DUKES!

TOUGH GUY!

F.G.W. #4

As a youngster growing up on the farm, I seem to recall a lot of bragging by certain individuals who thought they could "go you one better." Sometimes, this had to do with "fisticuffs" or other alleged manly prowess.

One that often "tickled my fancy" was: "I'm going to whip you within an inch of your life. Or, "I'm going to knock some sense into you!" (I wonder how you do that?) My Dad used to threaten us with this one when we misbehaved: "I'm going to flail the daylight out of you." He had one method that always got my attention. He would curl his middle finger under his thumb, and if he flicked you on your scalp, it really stung! Boy, I can still feel it!

I recall that when someone did something that we thought would get him into trouble with his parents, we would hear a couple of "zingers" like this: "Boy, your Dad is going to skin you alive" , or "Your Mom is going to peel your hide!" Now, wouldn't that be something to see? It hurts just to think about it!

One fellow used to scare the younger kids with "I'm going to whip you so bad that your own Mama wont recognize you." That would get my attention!

If a fellow was really tough he was said to be able to "whip his weight in alligators" or to "whip his weight in wildcats."

If you wasn't able to run away from a confrontation, the bad dude might try to scare you with "I'm going to stick to you like ugly on an ape" or "stink on a skunk."

If someone was bragging too much and he was challenged about his exploits, you might hear this remark: "I'd like to buy you for what you're worth, and sell you for what you think you're worth!"

Another good one is: "If you think I look bad, you should see the other guy." (This would likely follow a fight.) In order to try to raise your own expectations about an impending confrontation, you might say, "He ain't big, he's just tall, that's all." And, of course, "Grown men don't cry."

There were almost always some "friends" who wanted to "see some action." They would urge you to get into the fray with words like these: "I dare you! I double dog dare you!" Now, this was hard to ignore. After all, your manhood was at stake!

There was always someone in the background passing out observations such as: "If you can do it, it isn't bragging." Or, "If you've got it, flaunt it!"

No one wanted to ever hear these words: "He's a chicken" or "He's a 'fraidy cat'." or "He's lily-livered" or "He's a scaredy cat." This meant that you was thought to be a coward.

A comment that I once heard when two guys were testing each other's resolve was: "One of them is afraid of the other one, and the other one is glad of it!"

My Dad always told us boys never to start a fight, but if it was unavoidable, to "give a good account of yourself." He also said that if we got a whipping at school for some infraction, we could expect to get another whipping from him when we got home. (Does the term "double jeopardy" apply here?)

When someone was in really big trouble, and there wasn't much prospect of him escaping the inevitability of impending doom, he was said to be "hip deep in alligators!" Now, folks, that one codgers up an image in my mind that's down-right scary! Can you imagine being "hip deep" in alligators? Holy Toledo!!

If someone was undertaking a difficult task and it was still unfinished, it could be said that you wasn't "out of the woods yet!" This saying has to do with the difference between walking through a forest or woods as opposed to open fields. It is easy to get lost in the woods, whereas most folks can find their way in open fields. Thus, the unfinished task isn't over until it's over!

Anyone who was "feeling his oats" and thought he could whip anybody was said to be "too big for his britches!"

Whenever someone was "making a scene" and really acting up, he was said to be "having a tizzy fit!"

Occasionally someone would be bragging about some feat that he could supposedly perform. Sometimes, he would be challenged to do it, and he would renege. When this happened, he was said to have "cold feet!" It's a whole lot easier to talk about doing something than it is to actually do it.

Whenever something was obvious or easily discernible. it was said to be "as plain as day!"

If someone undertook to try to do something that he was obviously not able to accomplish, then he "wasn't cut out for it!"

To be in a place where there wasn't much light or outdoors at night when the moon wasn't visible, it was said to be "pitch dark!"

Someone who is a good "mixer" and willing to visit with "common folks" is said to be someone who is "down to earth!"

If you was dressed in your best clothing, you was said to have on your "Sunday go-to-meeting" clothes. ("Sunday go-to-church" clothes.)

When someone was faced with a difficult situation, and he kept his wits about him, he was said to be "as cool as a cucumber!"

A quaint way of saying that someone was busy was to say he was "busier that a one-legged man going up and down the stairs!"

"It's as lost as last year's Easter egg" meant that you had no idea where something was located.

To be really talkative, was to say that someone could "talk the horns off of a billy goat!" Or, "He could talk the legs off of a table!"

If you wanted to inform someone that you wasn't going to just sit idly by and not defend yourself, but you was going to take action, you might inform him of this by saying, "I'm going to cloud up and rain all over you!"

When you are pleased with the way things are, you are said to be as "happy as a June bug!"

There are times when someone is trying very hard to accomplish something and seemingly can't quite do it. And, to add to the frustration, the answer is right in front of him. When this happens, it is said that he "couldn't see the forest for the trees!"

When "dickering" with someone, and you wanted to quit "fooling around", and "get down to business", you would say, "Let's get down to brass tacks!"

To be without food or other necessities of life, and the situation was serious, you was said to be "down to the bare bones!"

Chapter 5

Sports and Sportsmanship

PLAYING MARBLES

I remember as a boy at home hearing the expression, "Faster than you can say, Jackie Robinson." This was a reference to the first African-American to play major league baseball. He was an excellent ballplayer and he was a very fast athlete. So, if someone was fast, he was compared to Jackie Robinson.

If someone broke the rules of sportsmanship, he was said to be "playing dirty pool." Remember when kids got together to play some game and the rules were almost always changed to fit the situation? Ah, the good old days!

I wonder what would happen if some announcer for the major leagues spoke of the teams during a game as being "in town" or "in the country?" Do you remember how it was decided who was to bat first? You would get a baseball bat, and someone would grasp it about half-way up, and someone from the opposite team would grasp it on the narrow end next to the first hand. This would continue until someone's hand covered the knob at the small end of the bat. That team got to bat first. That was the team that was "in town," while the other team went on defense and was said to be "in the country."

A common pastime in warm weather was to play horseshoes. This was done using actual horse shoes. Heaven help you if one of them ever hit you on the shin bone!

There were games that we played at night when all the chores were done. We would play both regular checkers and Chinese checkers. In the winter time we used to play Rook. Sometimes, when my older siblings came out to the farm, usually on Sunday, we would play Rook. I can still remember when my Dad was dealt the Rook, he would signal his partner in some manner that he had it. This, of course, gave them an edge. It was all in fun and some of those Rook sessions got really intense! How did we ever survive without television?

Did you ever play marbles? You would draw a circle in the dirt and place the marbles inside the circle. The object of the game was to knock the other player's marbles outside of the circle while maintaining your marbles inside the circle. Everybody had a favorite marble which was called a "taw."

How about mumble peg? This was played with a two-bladed pen knife. The long blade was opened all the way out, and the short blade was opened only half way. You would place the point of the long blade on the tip of the forefinger of your left hand and with your right hand you would flip it outward. If the knife landed with the long blade stuck in the ground, you got one point. If it landed with the short blade stuck in the ground, you got three points. If it landed with both blades stuck in the ground, you got five points. If it landed with neither blade stuck in the ground, you got no points. The one who got 21 points first was the winner.

Kids today with their electronic games, their I-Pods, their cell phones, their text messaging, their HD TV, their DVD's, etc. have no clue about the fun we had growing up in the '40s and '50s down on the farm!

How about this? I went into the Navy when I was 18 years old. I was in for four years. When I returned to the States from the Far East in 1956 at the age of 21, one of the first things I did was go to Nicholasville, my hometown, and take the driver's test for a driver's license. Can you imagine some 16 year-old being told today that he/she would have to wait until he/she was 21 to get their license? I bought my first car with money I had saved up each month in the Navy. For me to ask my parents to sign for me to get a driver's license or to ask them to buy me a car would have been ludicrous!

Do you remember deciding who would start some game by "drawing straws?" Do you remember "choosing up sides?" How one plays sports is a good indicator of one's character. What's in your heart will eventually come out through your mouth! An expression that I heard often at times like this was, "Cheaters never win!"

Remember "tag", "drop the handkerchief", "Rover, red rover", "pin the tail on the donkey", "follow the leader", "jumping rope", "bobbing for apples", "hide and seek", etc?

Can you recall going to someone's house for a birthday party when you was a teen-ager and playing "post office?" This was done with a group of boys and girls. You would sit on the floor in a circle and you took turns spinning a soda bottle. When a boy spun the bottle and it stopped and pointed at a girl, they both went into another room and kissed. The game stopped until both of them came back to the circle. Likewise, the same applied when a girl spun the bottle. If the bottle stopped spinning and was pointing at someone of the same sex, the bottle was spun again until it stopped at someone of the opposite sex. This was a popular game, let me tell you!

When we were young boys at home, my brother, Glenn, who was about 18 months older than me, and I used to take turns playing cowboys and Indians or a sheriff and some outlaw. Our imagination would allow us to pretend to be just about anybody we wanted to be. I can't imagine growing up with no brothers or sisters at home. Those were some good old days, let me tell you!

At about his earliest teen years, Glenn began drawing and sketching, especially sceneries and animals. I recall one pen and ink sketch that he drew of an elk that just about "blew us away", it was so good! He later taught himself to paint with oils. His specialty was animals that are native to the state of Kentucky. Some of his paintings are now hanging in a wide-spread area of the country. I have several in my home, and proud to display them.

If a couple got into a "scuffle", and the one who bested the other one did so without cheating, he was said to have won "fair and square." Anyone who got angry easily, was said to "fly off the handle."

When someone was involved in an athletic endeavor and his abilities were on display, his desire to excel was commonly referred to as "root hog or die!"

Speaking of fair play, the rules of sportsmanship should be the same for all participants. Country folks have a saying for this truth: "What's fair for the goose is fair for the gander!"

Folks that live in rural areas will use things they encounter regularly when describing happenings in their every-day life. For example, when someone is irritable or "out of sorts", he is described as having a "burr under his saddle!" Just imagine how uncomfortable it would be to a horse to have a burr under the saddle next to his skin when someone is riding on him. OUCH!!

Chapter 6

Am I Pretty or What?

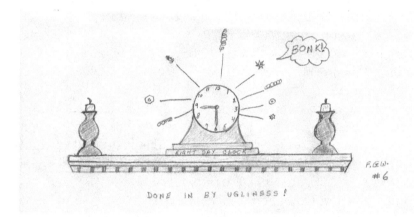

DONE IN BY UGLINESS!

Anyone who is vain about their appearance just might have a difficult time getting through life without encountering some "bumps" along the way. One expression that I've heard most of my life that captures the essence of this is, "She's as cute as a bug's ear." Think about that. How cute can a bug's ear be? It's not to be taken literally, of course, but it's an illustration of just how rare or seldom seen is her beauty.

Contrast that to the expression, "He was so ugly, they had to put a sack over his head when going out in public." Now that's not very nice, is it? How about, "You're so ugly that an ape looks like Clark Gable compared to you." (Clark Gable was a handsome movie star whom the ladies found irresistible during the '40s, '50s and '60s.) If you was thought to be really ugly, you was said to be "double ugly."

"Beauty is only skin deep, but ugly goes all the way to the bone." That one doesn't leave any wiggle room at all, does it? Mom would say, "Pretty is as pretty does." If someone was thought to be overly pampered, someone would surely say, "She's so sweet, honey wouldn't melt in her mouth."

Perhaps the insult of all insults concerning one's appearance is this one: "You're so ugly that your picture is beside the word 'ugly' in the dictionary!" Contrast that one with this one: "If I was any prettier, I'd have to wear a mask." If an ordinary citizen thought that he was as handsome as Clark Gable, he could be heard to say, "What's Clark Gable have that I don't have except a million dollars?"

Everyone wants to think that they are reasonably attractive. One way to have this prospect dashed is for someone to tell you, "You're so ugly, your face would stop an eight-day clock!" To fully appreciate this, you have to understand that an eight-day clock was a clock that was wound with a key, and it would tick-tock for eight days, come what may. So, if you was so ugly that it stopped an eight-day clock, you must have been really ugly! Another way of saying this was to say, "You're as ugly as a mud fence."

Talking about ugly, this one "takes the cake", "He's so ugly, his mother had to tie a pork chop on him to get the dogs to play with him." Now that poor fellow must have been a "doozie" if even the dogs wouldn't play with him without some incentive!

I remember when I was growing up on the farm hearing my Dad say, "There's no such thing as an ugly baby." To him, every child was someone special. He must have loved children, because he and Mom had ten of them! I still marvel at that.

No one with any sense of pride wanted to ever be called "Mama's little darling" or the "Teacher's pet." If you preferred to hang around your mother instead of playing with the other boys, you was said to be "tied to your Mama's apron strings."

And speaking of Mama, there was one thing that I remember vividly about Mom throughout the years that's "chiseled in stone" in my memory. Mom had very long hair most of her life. She would wash her hair and then go into the living room and sit in a straight-backed cane-bottomed straight chair and dry and brush her hair. When she sat in the chair, her hair would just about touch the floor. She would take a towel and rub her hair in the towel, first one side and then the other. Next, she would take her hair brush and brush out her hair until she had all the tangles out of it. Then, she would plait her hair into a single plait and tie off the lower end. This was how she prepared for bed. The next morning when she arose to start her day, she would wind the plait in a circular way and fasten it with long bobby pins at the back of her head. I can remember watching her as she did this and marveled at how beautiful her long hair looked.

But, alas, there came a time as Mom grew older that she confided to my sister, Mary, that she was considering cutting her hair because taking proper care of it was getting to be more than she wanted to do. I remember one day soon after that, Mary came by the farm and took Mom to town to a hair salon and had her hair cut to about shoulder length. I must confess that it took some getting 'used to' seeing Mom without her long hair. But, I'm sure it was considerably easier on her after that to take care of her hair.

Whenever Mom was going to be out-of-doors for any length of time, especially during the warm months of the year, she would wear a bonnet to protect her head from the heat of the sun. She had several of them and she would wash them and starch them. Then she would iron them and they really looked sharp on her when she wore them.

One expression that I've heard most of my life that conveys the fact that someone wasn't very good looking was to say that he or she was "as ugly as eight miles of bad road!"

To be in a situation where you was obliged to endure something unpleasant, with no way out of it, you was said to have to "put that in your pipe and smoke it!"

Chapter 7

Intelligence Quotient

In order to appreciate this area of interest, you must understand that there weren't too many Rhodes Scholars that came from "down on the farm." It wasn't unusual at all for folks to poke fun at each other concerning their "smarts." A good illustration of his fact is found in this little ditty: "Fool me once, shame on you. Fool me twice, shame on me."

All of my life I've heard this one. When asked why you did something, if you said "because", that wasn't a good answer. Either you knew why you did something, and you didn't want to reveal the reason, or you didn't know why you did something, and you didn't want to reveal you ignorance. I remember my Dad would get frustrated at us boys when we did something that didn't please him, and he would ask us why we did it. If we said "because", he wasn't a happy camper!

If you could "cipher", you was able to solve mathematical problems. I can still remember my teacher in elementary school. She made us memorize the "times table" until we could quote it up to 12 x 12. I really appreciate her insistence of this when I look back on it now.

Anyone who didn't have good common sense was said to be "dumb as a rock." If you couldn't understand something being said, it was said to be "Mumbo Jumbo."

One affliction that I had when growing up was to speak too fast. Mom used to tell me that her ears couldn't keep up with my mouth. In other words, "Slow down, Fred!" If the other person can't understand what you're saying, then you're not communicating, are you?

There were some quaint expressions that characterized this point. Among them were: "bumfuzzled", "bamboozled", "flim-flammed", "horn swaggled", "discombobulated", "hood winked", "taken to the cleaners", etc. Can't you just see someone sitting around thinking up these wonderful expressions?

If someone wasn't too bright, he was said to be " Crazier than a loon." Or, "He doesn't have the sense that God gave to a goose." Or, "He doesn't have sense enough to come in out of the rain." Anyone who was thought to be "weak in the head" was said to be "about two bubbles off-center!" This refers to a carpenter's level. When the surface that is being checked, either horizontal or vertical, is correct, the bubble will appear between two marked lines on the carpenter's level. Thus, if someone is "out of whack", the bubble will be off-center or outside of the two lines.

When questioned about a "bone-headed" mistake, you might reply, "I'm old enough to know better." Another good one is, "If brains were money, he'd be a pauper."

If you was unable to figure something out, you "couldn't tell which end was up." Mom used to describe someone who was really intelligent as "sharp as a tack!" If you was confronted with a problem and it was easy for you to solve it, finding the solution was said to be "as easy as falling off of a log!" Another quaint way of expressing this was to say that it was "as easy as shooting fish in a rain barrel." How about this one: "I know the question, what's the answer?"

I can remember my parents telling me when I was growing up not to let anyone "pull the wool over my eyes!" This had to do with someone trying to "pull a fast one on me." If someone was trying to "hoodwink" me by telling me some tall tale in an effort to trick me, he would be trying to "pull the wool over my eyes." So, I was cautioned to beware of this and to keep my wits about me.

Speaking of intelligence, a lot of our education came from the old Philco battery-powered radio. Remember, this was before we had electricity! We had to be conservative in how we used the battery, because we didn't want to run it down. Just remembering some of the radio programs brings back a flood of memories: "The Shadow", "Gang Busters", "The Lucky Strike Hit Parade", "Mr. & Mrs. North", "Sky King", "The Lone Ranger", "The Grand Ole Op'ry", "Just Plain Bill", "Fibber McGee and Mollie", "Amos and Andy", "George Burns and Gracie Allen", "The Jack Benny Show", "Sid Caesar", "The Old Time Revival Hour", "Bob Hope", "Milton Berle", "Friday Night Fights", and a host of others. Folks would gather around the radio and your imagination would take you wherever your mind would let you go! When compared to what's available on TV and other media outlets today, there is just no comparison.

Some of the newscasters of that era were: Gabriel Heater, Fulton Lewis, Jr., John Cameron Swayze, Walter Winchell, Lowell Thomas, Edward R. Morrow, and others. I remember that Dad would listen to the radio daily, especially during World War 2, and if there was dire news concerning the war, Gabriel Heater would begin reporting it by saying, "Folks, there's bad new tonight!" Then, he would proceed to report the news of how the war effort was progressing. He had a very distinctive voice, and in my memory I can still hear it.

As a youngster, I knew a fellow who talked a lot. He talked so much that he would get on people's nerves after a while. The best way to characterize this behavior problem would be to describe it this way: "His verbosity was exceeded only by his voluminous dialogue!" He was a talk-a-holic!

Can anyone explain to me why we park our vehicles in a "driveway", and drive across country on a "parkway?" Somehow, that seems backwards!

Why is it that we spell the words "four" and "fourteen" with the letter "u" in them, but when we spell the word "forty", we leave the "u" out? Go figure!

A not too gracious way of saying that someone isn't very smart is to say he "doesn't know the difference between his backside and a hole in the ground!"

When someone was looking for another person, and you hadn't seen him or didn't know where he was, you would say that you hadn't "seen hide nor hair of him!"

If someone was being lazy or doing nothing productive, it was said that he was just "piddling around!"

When something happened unexpectedly, it was said to have occurred "out of the blue!"

If you was truly startled about some event, you could be said to have had "the bejeebers scared out of you!"

For you to be able to perform some deed easily, while others struggled, it was said to have been done by you "in a cakewalk!"

To be going about from place to place with no purpose in mind was said to be "gallavantin' around!"

Chapter 8

The Good Old Days

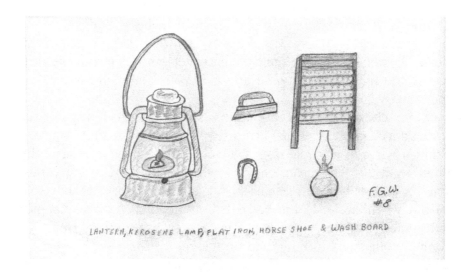

LANTERN, KEROSENE LAMP, FLAT IRON, HORSE SHOE & WASH BOARD

F.G.W. #8

Ah, yes, the good old days! A wonderful blessing of growing older is the joy of remembering things that happened "way back when." Things are so very much different now than, say, fifty years ago. That was before television, penicillin, polio vaccine and a host of other modern-day things that we now take for granted.

For example, I can remember back when I was in the fifth grade, and I was eleven years of age, that a man representing an electrical company came to our farm and asked my Dad if he would be interested in having electrical service ran to our house. Dad inquired about the cost and agreed to take it. It wasn't long after this that a construction crew installed power poles down our road and ran electrical wires from pole to pole. Those who had opted for the electrical service had wiring run from the nearest pole to the house. My Dad hired a cousin to wire the house for electricity. There were bare ceiling lights with pull chains to turn them on and off. I can clearly remember him telling us not to burn the lights any longer than necessary because it "cost money."

Try to imagine not having electricity and therefore no electrical appliances. We had an ice box instead of a refrigerator. Twice a week a man came around with an ice wagon and sold blocks of ice. My Dad would buy a block for our ice box at the house, and another one for the drink box at the store. One of the necessary jobs that had to be preformed regularly was to empty the drip pan at the bottom of the ice boxes. As the ice melted, the water ran down into the drip pan. If you forgot to empty the drip pan, you would have a mess on your hands!

Mom cooked on a coal-burning stove. She had a gasoline-powered Maytag washer that had a set of wringers on top to squeeze as much water as possible from the wet clothes. Then, of course, the clothes had to be hung out on the clothes line to dry. In the winter time the clothes would freeze as stiff as a board! Every Monday was wash day. The water had to be heated on the kitchen stove, summer and winter, in order to have hot water to wash clothes. Irons for ironing clothes had to be heated on the cook stove also. They were called "flat irons." Just about everything that was washed had to be ironed. This was before "wash and wear" or "permanent press" clothing was available. I can remember Mom heating the flat irons in the winter time and ironing the sheets at bedtime so they were warm when we went to bed. Central heat and central air! What's that?

There's one thing that stands out in my memory concerning Mom. Every day's routine was pretty much the same. The first thing she'd do after she got dressed for the day was to put on her apron. It was the type that covered her dress from the neck to the knees. It had a loop that went over her head and there were two straps that she'd tie in the back at the waist. Those aprons had pockets into which she placed various things that she needed as she went about her daily chores. That apron went on first thing in the morning, and it was the last thing to come off at night as she prepared to go to bed. Those aprons were a vital part of her daily routine. She used them for just about everything she did. It was an egg carrier when she gathered the eggs from the hen house. She carried vegetables and fruit in it from the garden and orchard. She used it to do a quick dusting of the furniture when company came unexpectedly. If it was meal time, she would wave it and we'd know it was time to go to the house to eat. It was useful for drying children's tears or blowing their noses into. She's wipe perspiration from her brow with it and it made a handy pot holder whenever she was handling something hot from the stove. And, of course, it protected the dress beneath it from getting stained or dirty.

I can still remember listening to the rain falling on the tin roof at bedtime. That was some of the sweetest sleep I've ever had!

A "poke" was your lunch sack. Our friends out West called their possessions when they traveled their "possibles."

Us farm boys always looked forward to Halloween so we could have some fun. It wasn't our nature to do any real damage, but we were mischievous none the less. About the best incident I know of was a group of boys took a farmer's wagon apart, put all of the pieces up on top of a tobacco barn, reassembled the wagon and left it there! The wagon straddled the peak of the barn roof and it caused quite a stir.

We would take farm gates and wooden outhouses and leave them a mile or so down the road. It's a wonder some of the boys didn't get shot for some of the pranks they pulled.

My grandfather Benton told me about something from his youth called "bundling." When a boy was "sparking" a girl in the late 1800s, there wasn't much to do in the winter time by way of entertainment. One thing that they could do if the girl's parents liked the boy who was "sparking" their daughter was to allow them to "bundle." This involved placing a wide board between them lengthwise from the headboard to the footboard of the girl's bed. There was a slot in the headboard and in the footboard that the bundle board fit into. They would lie down on their respective sides of the bundle board and pull the covers over them to keep warm. The idea was that they could spend some quality time together but not get into any "hanky panky." Remember, the houses were very cold away from the stove or fireplace. Usually, the bundling took place in the girl's bedroom, so the boy had to be of good character before the girl's parents would allow bundling to occur. The parents would, of course, check on them from time to time just to make sure!

As a boy on the farm I recall my father telling us from time to time during the growing season that we were going to "chop the corn" or "chop the tobacco." This was his way of saying we were going to go to the corn field or the tobacco patch with our hoes to chop down the weeds.

I can remember going to town every Saturday after lunch with Mom and Dad. We would be given a quarter. With that quarter we could buy a ticket into the "picture show", buy a bottle of pop, either a bag of popcorn or a candy bar for a nickel each, and still have four cents left over. The movie tickets cost eleven cents. After the show was over, we would go to the "five and dime" store and get four pieces of penny candy.

There was an event that happened to me in 1944 that made an indelible impression on me. I was with my Dad in front of the Nicholasville court house on Main Street. I was nagging him to buy me a pair of new shoes. He told me that he wasn't going to do so that day. I persisted until he finally told me this: "You think you really need a new pair of shoes. You don't know how lucky you are because you have two feet. There's a lot of people that's worse off than you think you are!" It wasn't five minutes after he said that to me that a service man (Army) came by on crutches that had one leg amputated at the knee. When I saw that, it brought a flood of emotions through me that I've never forgotten. I remember my Dad turned toward me and looked at me without speaking a word. It was as if he was reminding me of what he had just told me. WOW! I felt so ashamed!

Another experience that happened when I was twelve years old was just as valuable. I wanted a bicycle, but I knew that Dad wasn't going to buy me a new one. I did think that perhaps he might buy me a used one. I inquired around the neighborhood and learned that there was one for sale about two miles away for $11.00. When I asked Dad if he would buy it for me, he said, "Get a job and buy it yourself!" So, every night I would go to the grocery store he owned and I would ask the farmers if there was any work I could do for them so I could earn some money. Finally, one farmer told me he had a large field of corn that needed to be 'thinned.' In those days, the corn planters weren't very accurate. Sometimes, the planter dropped one kernel of corn, sometimes two, sometimes three, and sometimes a bunch. My job was to remove the excess stalks of corn at each 'hill'. I worked Monday through Saturday and was paid $2.00 per day for a total of $12.00. I walked to the bicycle owner's house, got the bicycle and brought it home. The chain was broken, the front tire was flat, and it needed new ball bearings for the front wheel. The next time we went to town, Dad helped me by buying the parts to get the bicycle ready to ride. I learned to appreciate that bicycle because I had worked at back-breaking work to get it!

Now-a-days, people go to the store whenever they want something. Years ago, it was common practice to swap for things. For example, if you wanted to buy a hog, you might offer the owner a sheep, or something else of equal value. If you didn't think you was being offered things of equal value, you might ask him to give you something "to boot." In our example, if the owner of the hog wanted more than your sheep for the hog, he might ask you to give him a rooster "to boot." There was a real art to this swapping business. You had to have nerves of steel and "stay your ground" in order to do well at trading.

Do you remember making snow cream after a fresh snowfall? How about home-made ice cream made with a lot of crank sweat? Did you ever have home-made caramel coated apples? Yummy!

Do you remember toasting yourself in front of a fireplace just before going to bed in the winter time? The bedrooms had no heat in them, and they were very cold in the winter months. Roast on the front and freeze on the back!

How about wearing "long handled" underwear with a "trapdoor" in the rear so you wouldn't have to take them off when you relieved yourself. In the winter time there was the old "slop jar", sometimes affectionately called the "thunder mug", that was placed in the bedroom so you didn't have to go to the outside to the outhouse!

Can you remember using the Sears and Roebuck catalog, or the Montgomery Ward catalog and others like that for toilet paper? People didn't waste good money buying toilet paper, for heaven's sake! Then, there was the spreading of lime down the "privy" to help keep the odor down in the summer time. Whew! You had to watch out for spider webs and spiders and snakes when you went to the outhouse.

I recall seeing Dad light the fire in the fireplace with a corn cob soaked in kerosene. One of my jobs at home before we got electricity was to trim the wick in the lamps, keep the lamp globes cleaned, and see that there was kerosene in the lamps.

Mom made our shirts, underwear, pajamas and other articles of clothing from feed and flour sacks. She made a truck load of quilts in her life time to help keep us warm in the winter. She embroidered, crocheted, knitted and did other needlework to help keep our home the best it could be. I got my first store-bought shirt when I was 16 years old!

Dad cut the boys' hair about once a month. He used a pair of scissors, a comb and a pair of clippers that were manually operated. Ouch! I can still feel it pulling my hair!!!!

Another thing Dad did was to remove the worn-out soles and heels from our shoes and put new ones on them. He had a set of shoe lasts that he used to accomplish this. You didn't stop using things until you had "gotten the good out of them."

I remember mowing our lawn with a push-type reel mower. Everything was fine until you got a stick or rock caught in the reel. You usually got a healthy poke in the stomach when this happened.

Our family had a reunion every summer, usually in June, when the crops were "laid by." One year there was about 100 or so present. Some of the food preparation was done out-of-doors and some indoors. By this time, some folks had indoor plumbing, and this left an impression on Grandpa Benton. I remember him saying, "What's this world coming to? Now-a-days the outhouse in inside, and they're cooking outside. What will they think of next?" Wouldn't he be surprised if he was here today?

Remember sitting in church or some other social event during the summer and fanning yourself with a funeral parlor fan? Remember going to church in the winter and having a pot-bellied stove in the middle aisle? Remember going to a tent revival in the summer?

Remember cultivating the crops with a mule and a double shovel plow? We had two mules at one time named "Beck" and "Red." If you wanted them to go to the right, you said "Gee", and if you wanted them to go to the left, you said "Haw."

Do you remember eating chicken and afterwards taking the wishbone, making a wish, and then pulling it apart? How it broke made all the difference in the world!

How many times have you been told that your hair looked like a "rat's nest" before you had a chance to comb it?

Remember when you had to change clothes and shoes when you got home from school or church because you didn't want to "wear them out?" Dad would buy us boys a pair of shoes just before school started in the fall, and that had to last us until next fall. So, we wore the old pairs of shoes, and we wore the patched clothing around the farm to conserve wear and tear on the newer ones. Pants and shirts were handed down from the older boys to the younger ones. The last four of us were boys, so you can imagine what they looked like by the time they got to me, the youngest!

In the days before automatic transmissions, if your battery was low, you always tried to park your vehicle on a slope so you could start it by letting it roll downhill and letting out the clutch pedal. This would turn the engine over and it would usually start.

When I first began to "fool around" with automobiles, they were very different from today's models. For example, the dimmer switch for the headlights was located on the left side of the floor board on the driver's side. Next, to the right was the clutch pedal (automatic transmissions weren't available yet). Next, to the right of the clutch pedal was the brake pedal. Next, to the right of the brake pedal was the accelerator pedal. Usually, up above and slightly to the right of the accelerator pedal was the starter switch. The car was started by pressing the starter switch with you right foot while simultaneously pressing the accelerator pedal. The ignition switch was located on the dashboard to the right of the steering column. The manual gearshift was located on the floor to the right of the driver. There was a long gearshift lever that was connected to the standard transmission and it was used to shift to either "low gear", "second gear", "third (or high) gear", and "reverse gear." The gearshift levers weren't moved to the steering column until the '40s. Now-a-days, some are back on the floor again!

In those days, there were no directional signal devices like on today's automobiles. You had to give manual signals with your left arm out the window instead. When it was cold or raining, it was a challenge, to say the least! To signal that you was going to turn left, you did so by sticking your left arm straight out the driver's side window. A right turn was signaled by the driver with his arm pointed up at the elbow. Slowing or stopping was signaled by pointing the left arm downward from the elbow.

Speaking of the "old days", do you remember when you had to have fender skirts for your car to be "cool?" How about curb feelers, steering wheel knobs, mud flaps, and a fox tail fastened to the upper end of your radio antenna? If you wanted to be really cool, you would get yourself a Continental kit. Now, that was really something! The other guys would be "green with envy!" Earlier, your car might have had a rumble seat or how about running boards? Anyone remember buying the whitewall rings that you put on blackwall tires to make them look like whitewall tires? If you really wanted to be "cool", you would have an outside sun visor installed. Your car was your status symbol. Remember "burning rubber?" Or, how about "peeling rubber?" Or, how about "scratching off?"

One thing I recall was that the windshield wipers were vacuum powered and when ever you was going uphill or the engine was "under a load", the wipers would stop moving because there wasn't enough vacuum then to power the wiper arms.

Trying to keep the windshield clear in cold weather was a challenge also. Heaters and/or defrosters weren't very reliable in the early days. Mostly, you had to keep a towel or cloth with you to wipe the inside of the windshield in order to try to be able to see how to drive. Looking back at it now, I'm amazed that there weren't more automobile wrecks due to poor visibility.

Another interesting fact about automobiles of that day was that you could get them in three colors: black, black or black! Also, I recall my Dad at one time owned a 1935 model four-door Chevrolet. The front doors were hinged on the front of the doors. The rear doors, however, were hinged on the rear of the rear doors and opened outward--just the opposite of today's models.

Since there was no central heat or air conditioning back then, you raised up the windows in the house in warm weather so you could get a cross breeze. In the winter time you had to keep opening the outer doors to a minimum. If you opened the doors excessively, you was sure to hear, "Close the door! Was you raised in a barn?"

Do you remember hearing your Mom or Dad telling you that you shouldn't cross your eyes? If you did so, they would probably tell you that they could get hung up that way! Remember hearing your parents tell you that if you played with fire, you would "wet the bed?"

And, absolutely no animals were ever allowed in the house! The house is not a barn!

One of my favorite radio programs that I listened to was called "The Suppertime Frolic." The host or emcee was a fellow by the name of Randy Blake. The program consisted mostly of country and gospel music. As I recall, there were a lot of commercials. I remember that listeners were encouraged to purchase items, and they were advised to send their requests for purchases to: "Suppertime Frolic, % WJJD, Chicago 1, Illinois." If the weather was stormy, the static noise would make listening to the radio a challenge.

Mom used to ask me to churn a jar of creamy milk so we could have butter. It would take about fifteen minutes of constant shaking before the butter appeared.

Did you ever get your pants' legs caught in the bicycle chain? That wouldn't make Mom happy!

One thing that I recall as a youngster was hulling walnuts in the fall. If you didn't wear gloves, you would have walnut stain on your hands, and it would take weeks before the stain disappeared.

Did you ever eat green apples before they ripened? If you did, you was sure to get "the green apple trots" You haven't lived until you've had the green apple trots!

I remember my Dad telling about the first time he saw an automobile up close in Estill County, Kentucky. He was riding in a wagon pulled by a team of horses. As they were going along, he heard this strange noise and it "spooked" the horses. Along came this car and Dad had his hands full controlling the horses. Can you imagine that?

Getting a telephone that was on a party line was an adventure! The way that you knew that the ringing of the phone was for you was by the particular signal the operator used. For example, at our farm house if the incoming call was for us, the operator would signal us with four "long" rings. There were a host of people along our road that were on the same party line. Interestingly enough, some of the folks along the party line liked listening in on other folks' phone calls. There was one "busy body" who liked to listen to other folks' phone calls, and you knew when she was "listening in" because you could hear her breathing on the line! This was impolite, it was an invasion of privacy, but she did so anyway. Dad played a trick on her one time while talking to someone else on the phone. Knowing that she was listening in, Dad began telling a really wild bit of gossip about a particular person. After a while, the gossip was all over the community, and before you know it, the "particular" person got in touch with the listener and gave her "what for!" If you had an emergency and you needed to call someone like a doctor or the fire department, etc, you would lift the receiver and tell the parties talking that you had an emergency and ask them to get off the line so you could call whoever you needed. In those days, there was an operator who made all the connections for incoming and outgoing calls. Whenever there was stormy weather, the phone service wasn't very reliable.

Mom used to mix the ingredients for biscuits every night, and put them in a bowl, cover them up with wax paper, put them in the refrigerator, and then bake them the next morning for breakfast. Nobody could make 'scratch' biscuits like Mom!

I recall when gasoline was 18 cents a gallon and kerosene was five cents a gallon. I remember the day a grocery salesman stopped at our store and left a few loaves of white, sliced bread. (It was called "light" bread.) It sold for eleven cents a loaf! Prior to this, most housewives baked their own bread at home.

I also remember the day a grocery salesman stopped at our store and left a few samples of "ready-made" cigarettes. They were ten cents a pack! Prior to this, most smokers used "roll your own" tobacco. A sack of "roll your own" tobacco cost five cents. Some of the more popular "roll your own" brands of cigarette tobacco were: "Buffalo", "Bull Durham", and "Duke's Mixture." There were cigarette papers that came with each sack of tobacco. Some folks could roll a fairly decent looking cigarette, but others didn't do so well. Shame on you if you tried to roll a cigarette when it was windy! The tobacco usually wound up getting blown all over the place. A popular brand of pipe tobacco was called "Prince Albert." A popular brand of chewing tobacco was called "Day's Work." Another one was called "Beach Nut."

I remember trying to chew some of Dad's tobacco that was hanging in the barn to cure. Since Dad had chewed tobacco all of his adult life, I figured I could do it too! That was my first mistake. I took some tobacco from a stalk of tobacco hanging in the barn and proceeded to chew it. After about five minutes I began to get about as sick to my stomach as I've ever been in my life! Needless to say, I never chewed tobacco again!

I can remember Mom coring apples, slicing them, and putting them on a sheet up on the roof of the summer kitchen so they could dry out. They would be used later to make pies or cobblers, etc. Yummy! And, her fried potatoes were simply great!

When I was about 13 or 14 years old, I wanted to make a banjo so I could learn to play it. I talked to Dad about it and he said that I would need a skin to cover the resonator in order for the banjo to have a decent sound to it. When I asked him what kind of skin I should use, he said a groundhog hide would work. Well, I had a .22 magnum rifle that I had been using to kill groundhogs with, so I figured that would be easy enough. Anyway, I proceeded to kill a ground hog, and then I began skinning it. That was about the most difficult job I ever got into. Ground hogs don't skin out very easily. Finally, I gave up and asked Dad what else we could use. He said that he would use a metal cake tin instead. He whittled out a neck for the banjo and fastened it all together and, wahlah! I had a banjo!

Another fascinating adventure I had was to buy a used Silvertone F-note guitar. I remember that I paid $3.00 for it! The only problem with the guitar was that it had a split down the middle of the back. This caused the strings to be about an inch above the fret board near the body of the guitar. It was impossible to play anything above the first four or five frets from the tuning keys. You talk about sore fingers! So much for that!

Do you remember boys combing their hair and having a "cow lick" in it? How about combing the hair on both sides toward the back of the head and ending up with a "duck tail" there? Grooming was so important to kids, especially teenagers. Remember "bobby soxers?" "Jitterbugging?" Remember the first time you heard Elvis singing "Blue Suede Shoes" or "Heartbreak Hotel?"

There was a drive-in theater on U.S. Highway 27 between Nicholasville and Lexington. It was a popular place for teenagers and young adults to frequent. There were, of course, always certain ones who would try to get into the theater without paying for tickets. Some would lie down behind the front seat covered with a blanket, etc. Some would hide in the trunk and try to get in that way. After a while, the management of the theater got wise to this and would look for these "cheapskates" as they entered the premises. Also, there were local law enforcement officials that patrolled the theater in an effort to "nip that practice in the bud." And, of course, the cars were checked from time to time to stop any "hanky panky."

Do you remember when church buildings didn't have a baptistery and folks who were converted to Christianity had to wait for warm weather so they could be baptized in a stream of water or a pond out-of-doors? This was especially true in rural areas.

When I was growing up and going to school, one of the things that most people took pride in was their penmanship. Penmanship was really stressed in those days. You must remember that in those days people communicated a great deal by writing. If someone didn't have good writing skills, his writing was said to be like "hen's scratching!" This was a reference to the antics of poultry when they're scratching in the ground with their feet looking for something to eat. I have noticed that school-aged children today as a rule don't have the quality of penmanship as their predecessors. Perhaps this is because penmanship is not stressed as much today. There are so many electronic devices in use today that people don't actually write as much as the previous generations.

When I was in the U.S. Navy during the Korea War period, I usually wrote to Mom and Dad about every day, and they would write to me about every day. I would recognize the hand writing the instant I saw the letters from home. It was reassuring to see them, and they played a vital role in my well-being in those days.

Sometimes in the summer months, us boys and a couple of neighborhood boys would go to the Kentucky River and camp out at a cave located above the river. We would put out a trot line across the river and bait the hooks and catch fish on them. We would take bedding to sleep on at the cave entrance and utensils to cook food with. It was quite an adventure. I can remember hearing all sorts of strange noises during the night as we tried to sleep. Of course, the older boys would tell all sorts of scary stories for my benefit. The trouble was, I didn't know whether to believe them or not!

One thing that I remember from the days that Dad owned and operated the grocery store concerned small children. Sometimes customers would come to the store accompanied by small children. It wasn't unusual for Dad to offer them a piece or two of candy. He had a glass cabinet that sat atop of the counter and anyone could readily see the various kinds of candy therein. If Dad saw a child looking longingly at the candy and it didn't look like the parent was going to buy any, Dad would sometimes offer the child some candy. Every now and then a child would say: "No, thank you." Whenever this happened, Dad would invariably say, "Well, if I can't give it away, there's no use in trying to sell it!"

It wasn't uncommon for Dad to dispense groceries "on the tab" to several of the local folks. They would buy groceries and promise to pay Dad when their crop, usually tobacco, sold in the winter. This worked out alright as long as they paid him when their crops sold. Sometimes, though, they didn't come in and pay like they promised. I know that after Dad passed away in 1970, there were about three shoe boxes full of tickets of grocery purchases by various people that had not paid as they had promised. Just before he died, Dad told my brother, Cornelius, Jr., the administrator of his estate, for him not to try to collect them. Junior took the boxes of tickets behind the house and burned them.

On another occasion when I was a young teenager, a farmer neighbor of ours lost his house in a fire. It was during the winter time and he, his wife, and two daughters, were able to escape the house with only their night clothes that they were wearing. A couple of days after that, I was over in the store with my Dad and that farmer came into the store. After a few minutes, I saw Dad take out his wallet and give the farmer a bunch of twenty-dollar bills. Dad told him that it wasn't a loan--that it was a "little something" to help him get back on his feet. After the farmer left, Dad told me never to mention what I had just witnessed to anyone--PERIOD! Dad didn't want to embarrass the farmer, and he didn't want to receive any acclaim for what he had just done. Needless to say, that left an impression on me for the rest of my life. It certainly gave me another insight into the many facets of my Dad's character.

Sometime around the late '40s we had a "bumper crop" of hay. Dad had cut the hay and we baled it and took it to the stock barn at the lower end of the barn yard. It was probably in late July and it was really hot! I remember the hay was put up in the barn loft above the stalls. This, of course, was the feed for the livestock for the up-coming winter. The stock barn had a tin roof on it and the hay was almost touching the tin. Evidently, the heat from the sun and the newly-baled hay next to the tin roof caused spontaneous combustion and the hay ignited and began burning. By the time Dad became aware of the barn being on fire in the loft area, it was already too fully engulfed for him to put it out. I remember that he finally had to jump out of the loft area at the front of the barn and he had burned both of his arms fighting the fire. Boy, that had to hurt!

For the next several days, Dad would take a note pad and he figured up the materials list of what he needed to replace the stock barn. When he had concluded what he needed, he got in touch with someone up in Estill County and ordered the lumber he needed from a sawmill there. After a few days, a truck brought a big load of lumber to our farm and it was off-loaded. I recall that Dad worked for a few days notching the long beams to accommodate the bracing pieces. Next, he poured the foundation and then proceeded to build the new stock barn. Things like this you never forget!

Another event that I clearly recall was also in the late '40s. It was in the winter time and there was ice and snow on the ground. Mom had gone outside the back kitchen door and was attempting to go up into the back yard. In order to do this, she had to step up two steps to the ground level. Something caused her to lose her footing and she fell down. In doing so, she broke her ankle and it was crushed. She had to be taken to the doctor and pins and screws had to be inserted to hold the ankle together until it mended. I remember that her ankle was swollen for a great length of time. She suffered through much pain for a long time after that. Incredibly, Mom continued with her daily chores and activities. She put a crutch under her arm and hobbled around the best she could. Mom was as tough as "whang leather!" What an inspiration to us boys! Also, she had a pronounced limp for the rest of her life because of it.

When I was about ten years old, I recall that my Dad asked me to go with him to the back part of our farm. At this particular part of the farm there was a grove of trees and a sinkhole. Dad wanted to recane the bottom of some straight-back chairs and he needed to get some tree bark for that purpose. We came upon some hickory trees that were about six or eight inches in diameter. Dad proceeded to take his knife and cut into the bark in a vertical manner about ¾ of an inch wide all around the tree trunk up to about six feet high. Next, he cut around the base of the tree and then proceeded to strip the bark off. Then, he took it to the house and let it soak in water until it was soft. When he was ready to recane the chairs, the hickory was soft and pliable. After he had finished caning the chairs, the bark began to dry out, and when doing so, the bark began to shrink. This, of course, made the cane bottom of the chairs tighten up. Dad was very good at this sort of thing and I marveled at his ability to do things like that with his hands.

One year Dad grew some sugar cane on our farm. When it was ready to harvest, it was cut and "shocked" similar to the way corn was harvested. Then, the cane stalks were taken to a cane press. There, a mule would walk around in a circle with his harness fastened in such a way that it would turn the gears that forced the liquid out of the sugar cane stalks. The liquid would then drain down a chute into a large vat. Beneath this vat was a fire that cooked the liquid. The liquid had to be stirred regularly and skimmed across the top to remove the foam. Eventually, the liquid reached the desired texture and you had molasses. Let me tell you, there's nothing better than molasses on a hot biscuit with butter on it! Yummy!!

I remember going with Mom to a field on our farm where there were some sassafras bushes. We would dig up some of the roots and put them into a bucket we had with us. When we got back to the house, Mom would clean them and cut them into strips. Next, she would boil them in hot water and the finished product was sassafras tea. Boy, that was tasty! This is another example of how you made use of whatever was available to eat on the farm.

I recall that Dad sowed leaf lettuce seeds in a lettuce bed that was covered with a piece of tobacco bed canvass in early March. Then, when the lettuce was ready, he liked to put it on his plate and pour hot bacon grease on it. To him, that was some fine eating!

Every summer around the first of July, we would go to several blackberry patches on our farm and gather several buckets of blackberries. Mom would make pies, cobblers, or put them over bowls of cereal. The rest she made into jams or jellies or preserves.

Likewise, we gathered strawberries every year, usually in May. One year Cornelius, Jr. planted a field of strawberries as a source of income. That was quite an undertaking for him. I remember he had to protect the plants with straw in the winter.

Mom sold whatever eggs that we didn't eat ourselves, and the extra milk from the cows was sold to a creamery. This was Mom's source of spending money. She called it her "milk and egg" money. Can you imagine what it must have been like trying to raise ten children on a farm in those days? The more I think about it, the more amazed I am at what Mom and Dad accomplished.

The next time you drink a glass of milk or pour cream into your coffee, thank a dairy farmer. I've always thought that the closest thing to being in jail for a farmer was to be a dairy farmer. The cows have to be milked twice a day, seven days a week, twelve months a year, come what may. That doesn't leave much time to go anywhere for an extended length of time, because the cows have to be regularly milked and tended to.

Of all the things that had a profound influence on me as I was growing up, certainly one of them was the sound of Mom singing hymns as she went about her daily chores. I can still hear her singing, "Rock of Ages", "The Old Rugged Cross", "Jesus, Lover of My Soul", "What a Friend We Have in Jesus", "In the Garden", and "Mansion Over the Hilltop", to name a few. Of their ten children, three of Mom's and Dad's sons were preachers and one daughter was a Sunday School teacher. I've always been thankful for my parents and the home environment that I was exposed to while growing up.

Many of my siblings could play musical instruments. Ruth didn't; Carl played the fiddle; Tootsie played the mandolin; Russell didn't; Audrey didn't; Mary played piano; Virgil didn't; Junior played the "violin"; Glenn played the guitar; and I played the piano, the harmonica, the guitar, and the mandolin. Dad played the fiddle and the banjo. Mom played the piano. Tootsie's husband, Carter Lowry, played the fiddle and mandolin. Later, their son, Jerry Rice, learned to play the guitar. It wasn't unusual at all for us to "make music" whenever we got together. That was some of the most enjoyable times that I had growing up on the farm.

All five of my own children were musically inclined. Gary, the oldest, played the piano and was church pianist on several occasions. Wayne, the second-born, plays the piano, guitar and bass guitar. Donna, the third-born, played the piano and had a lovely alto voice. Denise, the fourth-born, plays the piano. Kevin, the last-born, plays all of the percussion instruments, and received a music scholarship to attend college.

Christmas time around our farm was always exciting. I can vividly remember us boys and Dad going back over the farm looking for a cedar tree to be cut and decorated in our farm house. There were green and gold and red stringers that were wrapped around the tree. Sometimes, Mom would pop some popcorn and these would be stringed with a needle and thread and placed on the tree.

Some of the gifts that I received as a youngster at Christmas time were a pocket knife, a harmonica, gloves and things like that. One year Dad made me a slingshot that he made himself. He found and cut a "Y" shaped slingshot from a tree limb and some half/inch strips of rubber from an old inner tube. Next, he cut out a piece of leather from the tongue of an old shoe. He fastened it all together and it was really great. I recall that Dad cautioned me not to shoot at any animals, such as birds, etc.

One Christmas Eve when I was nine years old, Mom was busy wrapping gifts for family members not living at home with us. She needed her fountain pen so she could write their names on the tags. She asked me to go into her bedroom and get her pen that was on the dresser. I went into her bedroom and neatly stacked along one wall was a large number of sacks that had apples, oranges, grapes, candy, chewing gum, etc. Each sack had the name of a family member pinned at the top. It was then that I suddenly realized that what I had been told for years about Santa Claus wasn't quite true! Boy, was I crushed. When I took the pen to Mom and told her what I had discovered in her bedroom, she was really flustered. I think she was as disappointed as I was. In the rush of the moment, she had simply forgotten that the sacks were in there. But, I survived!

Speaking of fountain pens, do you remember those fountain pens that had a bladder in them? You would pull the lever up and stick the fountain pen into a bottle of ink, and slowly move the lever back to its original position. In doing so, you filled the bladder with ink, and then you could write with it until all the ink was used up in the pen. Do you remember what happened when the bladder leaked? You would have a nice big ink spot in your shirt pocket. I don't know how many white shirts that I saw years ago that had ink spots on them because of a leaking fountain pen! Thank heavens for ball point pens!

When you wanted to look your very best, or when you wanted to make a good impression on others, you was said to be "putting your best foot forward."

If you was attempting to accomplish something and it didn't turn out quite like you wanted it to, you might express your displeasure by saying, "Well, fiddle-dee-dee!"

Someone who got mad about something and couldn't control his temper was said to be "hotter than a firecracker!" Another way of expressing this was to say that the angry person was "madder than a wet hen!" There are at least two animals that don't like to get wet: a cat and a hen. A cat or a hen will get downright frantic when they get wet. So, if you have trouble controlling your temper, you are said to be "madder than a wet hen."

I remember there was a fellow that my Dad would hire from time to time to help with the farm work. It was Dad's custom to furnish the noon meal to anyone that was hired to help us. This particular fellow had a tremendous appetite and could really "put away the chow." Dad used to say that this fellow would "eat anything that didn't eat him first!' One time Dad said that this fellow was "going to eat him out of house and home!"

And, speaking of meals, down on the farm the noon meal at home was called "dinner", and the evening meal was called "supper." "City slickers" called the noon meal "lunch", and the evening meal was called "dinner." So, if you was going to join them for a meal at either noon or in the evening, you had better "nail down" which meal they meant. Otherwise, you just might show up at the wrong time!

There was an elderly gentleman and his grandson who would come to Dad's store about once a week and buy groceries. They would bring an empty potato sack and ride to the store on a mule. After the purchases were made, the groceries would be put inside the potato sack and tied off at the open end. When the grandfather got upon the mule, his grandson handed the sack of groceries up to him. Instead of straddling the sack over the mule's back, the grandfather put it upon his shoulder. When asked why he didn't put it on the mule's back, he said that the mule "already had enough to carry without adding to it!" I remember that my Dad just stood there and shook his head and tried not to laugh!

Over the years, Dad's store was broken into several times. In order to discourage this from happening, Dad would keep a dog tied to the outside of the rear of the store. I can remember at lunch time, Dad would take two slices of bread and put pinto beans and fried potatoes on them and he'd take it to the store and feed it to him. He had one dog by the name of "Bullet" that I recall was a good watch dog. But, after eating those sandwiches, he'd be so full of gas that he was miserable. I can remember whenever I was near him that I could hear him moaning something awful! And, it was hard to get close to him because the air was "green" from the gas he was passing! Memories are made of this!

Anyone who was well off financially was said to have "more money than Carter has liver pills!" Years ago on the radio, one of the products that you heard advertised often was that of Carter's Little Liver Pills. The pills were small and just about "every time you turned around", you would hear one of Carter's commercials. And, anything that was plentiful was compared to Carter's Little Liver Pills! ("He's got more troubles than Carter has liver pills!", etc)

Whenever someone came along and wanted to join in with those who had been involved with something for a length of time, he was said to be a "Johnny-Come-Lately!" Sometimes those who had been there for some time would be jealous of the "newcomer."

If a group of people were united in a common cause, especially if it was for some illegal activity, those involved were said to be "as thick as thieves." On the other hand, if "the going got tough" for folks engaged in illegal activities, and it looked like they might get caught, it would usually be "everyone for himself." In that case, there would be "no honor among thieves!" They would "run like rats from a sinking ship!"

Sometimes folks got involved in some endeavor, and it seemed that the harder they tried, the worse it got. It's almost like they took two steps forward and slid back three. In that case, they were said to be "hanging on by a tooth and a nail!" This could also be said for anyone who had little or no money, and they were faced with a lot of expenses with little prospect of being able to come up with the money.

Did you ever play "hop scotch" when you were a child? Country folks might have a harder time finding a suitable place to draw the squares than city folks who had sidewalks they could use. Have you ever figured out why you was told not to "step on the cracks" in a sidewalk?

How about when a black cat crosses in front of you? Or, walking underneath a raised ladder? Or, when Friday, the 13th comes around? Or, being sure that you exit a house by the same door that you entered the house, especially on New Years Day? And, speaking of New Years Day, you wanted to be sure that you ate some black eyed peas on that day! If you broke a mirror, you was sure to have seven years of bad luck!

There was always some home remedy for just about any ailment that could befall you, and there usually was someone in the community who could "prescribe" something for whatever your malady was. (Roots, herbs, etc) We've come a long way!

Another recollection I have of my "growing up" years on the farm occurred each spring. My parents would order some baby chicks early each spring, and they would be delivered to our farm by the rural postal carrier. They were so cute, soft as a feather, and cuddly. I remember they were shipped in a cardboard box that had round holes in the top so they could get oxygen to breathe. Mom would put them in a "brooding" house that had an electrical light bulb to generate enough heat to keep them warm until such time as the weather warmed up. There was a long feed trough which contained chicken feed. There was also a container which had water in it for the chicks. These chicks would, of course, be our future source of eggs and some would be killed and dressed for meat for meals.

In the days before my parents ordered baby chicks through the mail from a poultry hatchery, they would get a new "crop" of chicks the "old fashioned" way. I can remember them "candling" eggs. Candling was done by checking each egg individually with a light.

The light would be placed behind the egg in such a way as to make a primitive "xray" of the eggs. Those that would become baby chicks were set aside from those that would not. Then, the eggs that were selected for hatching would be placed in a hen's nest in the hen house, and a hen would sit on them for several days until they hatched. After the chicks hatched, that mother hen would stick with them like "warts on a frog" as they were growing up. She would teach them to hunt for food, warn them when danger came near, and she would protect them from rain and other harmful events. The sight of a mother hen with her brood of chicks under her wings is one that I shall never forget. Farm life has its own rewards!

Farm life was a series of cycles. Baby animals, such as calves, lambs, pigs, and chicks would be born in the springtime as a rule. The crop land and the garden area had to be plowed under, and the soil prepared for planting of vegetables and cash crops. They all had to be tended to as they grew to maturity. The soil had to be cultivated and weeds hoed so the plants could get as much nutrition from the minerals in the soil as possible. When the hay was ready, it had to be mowed, baled and taken to the barn. The tobacco and corn had to be harvested. Preparation for the winter months had to be done properly in order to get ready for the next year when the cycle started all over again.

There was always work to be done, and weather played an important part in the success of farming. I remember Dad used to say that the weather was one aspect of farming that a farmer had no control over. He listened every day to the weather forecasts and he kept an "eye to the sky" regularly. Farmers' livelihood depended upon the condition of the crops at year's end. There was very little income coming in during the growing season. The "pay day" came when he took the crop to market and received the monetary reward for his labor. Farming is not for the "faint-hearted!"

Back years ago before the days of permanent press or wash-and-wear clothing, sometimes when certain articles of clothing were laundered, starch would be added to make the articles smoother and more presentable when ironed, such as shirts, etc. One interesting by-product of this effort had to do with a person's appearance when he wasn't happy about something. When folks did the laundry, they would never add starch to their underclothing. This would make underclothing virtually impossible to wear. So, if someone had a "long face" and didn't seem too happy, it was said that they must have had "starch in their underwear!" Only someone who has lived through this era can really appreciate this saying! (Starch in underclothing would make them stiff and uncomfortable!)

Say, how long has it been since you've smelled the fragrance of a honeysuckle vine? Every spring and summer, one of the great blessings of being raised in the country is to be able to smell the honeysuckle vines.

As a boy on the farm, I enjoyed watching honey bees as they went from blossom to blossom and gathered nectar. When they had enough nectar, they would make a "bee-line" back to the hive and deposit it into the honeycomb and, "presto", you had honey. Did you know that without bees, there would be no fruit, because the bees spread the pollen around that enables the fruit to reproduce? No bees, no fruit!

Can you remember years ago when you drove into a "filling station" to buy gas? The attendant would ask you if you wanted "regular" or "ethyl.." While the tank was being filled, the attendant would clean your windshield, raise the hood and check the fluid levels, check the condition of the wiper blades, and check the tire pressure in your tires. Back in those days, they were called "service stations!"

I recall that Dad had a gas pump at his store. It had a glass compartment at the top that would hold ten gallons. There was a marker that showed the amount of gas that was put into the customer's vehicle. The gas had to be pumped up from the underground tank to the top of the pump with a lever that you moved back and forth. When you put the hose nozzle into the customer's gas tank opening, gravity would feed the gas as long as you held the nozzle lever open.

Years ago, merchants lured you to their places of business by offering you "S & H Green Stamps" or with "Yellow Stamps." Usually there was a redemption store nearby where you could redeem your books of stamps for merchandise that you selected from a catalog that the redemption stores furnished. The times have certainly changed!

Back in the days of kerosene lamps, if someone got between you and the lamp, it would create a shadow. When that happened, you were sure to hear this: "Move, you're in my light!"

Anyone who kept an appointment without being late was said to be "Johnny on the spot!"

Remember the "good old days" when you would hang "fly paper" strips to catch flies. For every fly that was stuck on the paper, there seemed to be four to take its place! How did we ever survive?

Chapter 9

How's That Again?

PUTTING THE FOX IN CHARGE OF HEN HOUSE?

It is wonderful how country folks can come up with some statement, words of wisdom, wise cracks, and other assorted linguistic offerings that will "tickle your funny bone."

If someone is bashful or shy and isn't forth-coming when spoken to, he might hear this question: "Has the cat got your tongue?" This is especially true with young children.

When someone doesn't look well he is said to "Look like death warmed over." I'll bet that made somebody's day when told that!

If clothing didn't fit because it was too small, it was said to be "Tighter than Dick's hat band." The same would apply if someone was stingy with their money.

How would you like to be told that you was "Dumber than a Missouri mule?" I don't know what it is about mules from Missouri that makes them dumb, but I've heard that expression from my earliest childhood.

When someone did something really stupid, that was like "Putting the fox in charge of the hen house." That's not very bright, is it? How about: "There's no use in closing the barn door after the horse gets out?"

An expression that I've heard all my life is when a youngster is getting a spanking for misbehaving (spanking: what's that?) is: "This is going to hurt me more than it does you." At the time, I found that one hard to believe. But, as a parent, I must say that I now agree with that one.

How about this one: "Don't confuse me with the facts. My mind is already made up?"

Another jewel is: "The hurrieder I go, the behinder I get." (Say what?)

If someone was really old, he was said to be "Older than dirt," or "Older than the hills." Another quaint way of expressing this same truth was to tell him, "You're older than Methuselah." (969 years.)

If someone wasn't too bright or seemed to be behind the times, he might be told: "Did you just crawl out from under a rock?" Or, "Who do you think you are, Rip Van Winkle?"

One that I like concerns a child who has a case of the giggles. You might tell him that his "giggle box has overturned and all of his giggles are falling out!"

If someone was stingy with his money, he was said to be so tight that he "squeaked when he walked."

This one "takes the cake": "If I've told you once, I've told you a million times…" (Really, a million times, eh?)

The usage of pronouns was really butchered something awful.

Some classic ones are: "We'uns"=all of us; "you'uns"=all of you; "You all" (y'all)=all of you, etc.

When I was pastor of a church down in Tennessee in the '70s, a fellow came to my house one day and asked me if I would "carry" him to town. It took me a few minutes to understand that he wanted me to drive him to town! Down there folks would use the word "hope" instead of "help." That took some getting used to also. If someone offered to help you do something, he would say: "Can I hope you?" If you wasn't sure about something, you would say: "That's a definite maybe."

I remember when it was bedtime at home on the farm that Mom would tell us that "It's time for us to go to bed so the rogues can have a chance." Another way of saying that you was going to "call it a day" and go to bed was to say that you was going to "hit the hay," or you was going to "hit the sack!" And, speaking of bed, if you made a bad choice and you got caught, you usually would be told: "You've made your bed, now sleep in it!" Folks learned early on in life that you take responsibility for your decisions.

Folks who seemed to be habitually "out of luck" might exclaim that "bad luck follows me around like a dark cloud." And, if someone was confronted with a very difficult situation, and there didn't seem to be any way out of it, he was said to be "up a creek without a paddle!"

If something didn't sit too well with you and you wanted to express your displeasure at someone, you might tell him to "Kiss my foot!" (Nice folks didn't mention other areas of their body.)

If someone was really poor or strapped for money, he was said to be "Too poor to even pay attention!"

If something wasn't likely to happen, you might hear: "Hell will freeze over before that happens." Or, "That has about as much chance of succeeding as a snowball in hell."

One expression that I've heard that isn't really nice concerns a cemetery. One fellow was heard to say, "People are just dying to go there."

When some local person thought he was as good as some famous person such as a movie star, or famous singer, etc. you might hear something like: "Eat your heart out, _____ _____!" (Insert famous person's name.)

Sometimes things would be happening around you and you didn't want to get involved with them. You would say: "It's no skin off my nose." Or, "It don't make me no never mind!"

If someone called you a "polecat" or a "skunk", you certainly was not being complimented!

Polite or nice folks didn't speak about someone's backside in plain English. When you found it necessary to speak of this you might word it like this: "The north end of a duck flying south", or something similar.

Growing up on the farm brought forth a multitude of scrapes, bruises and contusions. When this happened, you always wanted to have mercurochrome used on the cut instead of iodine. Why? Because iodine stung like "all get out" compared to mercurochrome.

I remember when I was about twelve or so, it was tobacco-cutting time on our farm. Along with my Dad and brothers, I was cutting tobacco and spearing it on a stick. You would grasp a tobacco plant, which was about head high, and bend it over and cut it off a few inches above the ground. To cut the plant, you used a tobacco knife which was called a "tomahawk." As I was proceeding down the tobacco row, I was cutting a tobacco plant and instead of hitting the plant with my tomahawk, I cut my left hand on the back of my hand and thumb. Well, it bled like something fierce. When I informed my Dad, he came over, took out his red handkerchief, put his chew of tobacco in it, and wrapped my cut hand with it and told me to go to the house and "See your Mama!" That was that!

Do you remember castor oil? On one occasion Mom had prepared hominy along with other vegetables for lunch. I didn't want to take any on my plate when the bowl was passed around the table. My Dad informed me that unless I took some and ate it, I would have to take some castor oil instead. It's really amazing how quickly I acquired a taste for hominy that day! We were told that we couldn't be "picky" about the food we ate. We could put as much food on our plate as we wanted, but we had better eat what we did put on it. Simple farm economics!

If you needed to excuse yourself so you could go to the toilet, you would say: "I've got to go see a man about a horse."

You never said that a lady was pregnant. You would say that she was "In a family way."

Of all the colloquialisms, funny sayings, witticisms, and down-right hilarious bits of folk lore that I've heard throughout my lifetime, the one that "takes the cake" for me is this one that has to do with leaving the house and going somewhere out in the public. Just as sure as God made little green apples, as we were leaving the house, Mom would tell us boys, "Be sure you've got on clean underwear in case you're in a wreck!" Now, folks, I want you to think about that one! "Be sure you've got on clean underwear in case you're in a wreck!" In every incidence of vehicle wrecks that I know anything about, I've never heard anyone, either victims or rescuers, say anything about whether the victims had on clean underwear or not! I think it has to do with personal hygiene and being sure that we had on clean clothes. I've pondered that one for years! There were ten of us children in our family, and it was important to Mom that we were clothed in presentable clothing.

I can honestly say that we never wanted for food or any other necessity when we were growing up on the farm. We had a large-sized garden and a large orchard that had apple, peach, pear, and plum trees. There were blackberry patches and strawberry patches on the farm. Mom made jams, jellies and preserves from the fruit, as well as canning many of the vegetables that were grown in the garden. Much of the clothing we wore as children was made by Mom on her Singer sewing machine. Also, we raised hogs and chickens for meat.

There was always plenty of chores that had to be done in order to keep everything going. I had two cows that I had to milk every morning and evening. Eggs had to be gathered daily, water buckets had to be kept filled, coal and kindling had to be kept in the house in the winter time and the livestock had to be fed on a regular basis. The crops had to be taken care of throughout the growing season. Hay had to be cut, raked and baled during the summer. During the winter, ice on the pond had to be broken so the livestock could get drinking water.

When the crops were "laid by", us boys could "hire out" to other farmers. I recall that I hired out one summer to a fellow who owned a thrashing machine. Usually, a combine machine would cut the wheat and it would be tied in bundles. Then, a thrashing machine would be used to separate the wheat grains from the stalks. My job was to be the "sacker." As the grains were being separated from the stalks, the grains would be diverted through an area to where grain sacks were fastened to catch the grain. There would be two sacks fastened and a diverter would direct the grain toward one of the sacks. When one of the sacks was filled, the diverter would direct the grain toward the other sack. While the second sack was being filled, the first sack would be disconnected, tied off, and an empty sack put in its place. This back and forth maneuver went on until all the wheat had been thrashed. One thing I remember about that job: it was a dirty, dusty job!

Another job that I did during the summer months was working with a stationary baler. My job was as the "blocker" and "wire poker." Whenever there was enough hay in the baler to make a proper sized bale, a block to separate the bales had to be put in place. Then, the two wires that were used to hold the bales together had to be "poked", or put in place. When the second block was put in place, then the ends of the two wires were fastened together. As the bales were forced through the baler, they would drop off at the end onto the ground ready to be picked up, loaded on a wagon or truck, and taken to the barn. This was hot, dirty and noisy work. One time I was poking wires for a bale and as I reached down to begin poking the wire, a snake was hissing at me! It had been raked up with the hay and placed along with the hay into the baler. It was forced along the way with the hay and it couldn't get loose to escape. That was interesting!

I remember going with Dad to the corn field around Thanksgiving time to "shuck" corn. The corn crop had earlier been cut and tied together into shocks. A "shock" was sixteen hills of corn with the middle four hills being where the "shock" was started. The four hills of corn were bent and tied together and the rest of the hills around them were cut and leaned up against the middle four hills. Then, when you had a "shock" full, it was tied with twine. In November Dad and I or some of my brothers would go to the corn field, disassemble the shocks and remove the ears of corn from the stalks. We would "shuck" the corn (remove the shuck from around the ear of corn) and pitch the ear of corn onto the wagon. When we got a load of corn, we would take it to the corn crib and shovel the corn into the crib. As you can imagine, it would be very cold and sometimes there would be snow on the ground. Our feet and hands were "cold as the dickens!" But, the livestock had to have food to eat, especially in the winter.

There were a lot of chores on the farm that were done by hand that machines do now-a-days. Many modern-day machines save countless hours of hard, back-breaking labor that we were required of necessity to do the "hard way!" Back then it was truly "sun up to sun down" just to try to keep up with all that had to be done. But it was a good life.

I remember one time in early spring that us four boys were up in the tobacco barn playing "follow the leader." The tobacco barn was about five rails high and at the peak or center of the inside of the barn it was a "fur piece to the ground" from the top rail. What us boys would do is: one of us would start out climbing the rails, up and down, back and forth, and the rest of us would have to follow him. Heaven help us is any one of us had fallen out of the barn. Mom and Dad would have "skinned us alive!" It's a thousand wonders that one of us didn't get hurt. But, this was just another example of our "home grown" entertainment! When I look back on it now, I can't help but wonder just how we kept from killing ourselves with some of the antics we pulled off.

Workmanship and pride in one's work was an inherent trait with folks who labored to make a living using their abilities. If something passed the test of time and usage, it was said to last "till the cows come home!" This, of course, meant that it was of good quality and could be expected to be useful a long time.

Sometimes folks had to choose between two or more choices around the farm. If it really didn't seem to make much difference which one was chosen, it was said to be "six of one or a half dozen of the other!" In other words, it didn't really matter which one was chosen because the outcome would probably be about the same.

An example of how country folks used certain expressions to discuss taboo subjects is like when we were in the barn yard and we stepped into a "fresh" cow patty. Instead of saying that we had "stepped in cow manure", we would say, "I cut my foot!" Now, doesn't that sound much nicer? Mom used to tell us boys when we were coming into the house after having been in the barn yard, "If you've 'cut your foot', take your shoes off before you come in the house!" Also, if it had been raining, and it was muddy, Mom would admonish us not to "track mud" into the house. We were told in no uncertain terms that we were to clean the mud from our shoes before entering the house.

If folks were happy and contented with their circumstances in life, they were said to be "as happy as a bug in a rug," and if you was really comfortable, you was said to be "as snug as a bug in a rug!"

When someone was stingy or "tight" with their money, trying to get them to part with it was said to be "like trying to get blood out of a turnip!"

If you didn't understand something that was being discussed, it was said to be "about as clear as mud!"

While attempting to do something for yourself, and the more you tried to do so, the worse it became, you was said to "shoot yourself in the foot!"

When someone was trying to teach someone else how to do something, and there wasn't much progress being made, it was said to be like the "blind leading the blind!"

How about "happy as a lark" or "dumb as a fence post?" Just how smart can a fence post be, anyway?

When you wanted to tell folks that some place wasn't very far away, you would tell them that it was only "a whoop and a holler away!"

If something was costly and it was thought to be exorbitant in price, it was said to cost "an arm and a leg!"

When you was trying to complete some task and you either didn't have time to properly finish it, or you just didn't "have the heart" to put much effort into it, it was said that you only gave it a "lick and a promise!"

Sometimes folks wouldn't be trying very hard to work. In that case, you was sure to hear someone say, "Get a little life about you!" Or, "Get a move on!" Another quaint way of saying this was to tell them to "shake a leg!" Our friends out West would word it like this: "Rattle your hocks!" Out West, in days gone by, the cowboys spent a lot of time around horses. When horses are walking, the hock area (similar to human's ankles) produces a sound much like that of a rattle. Thus, when you want to get them to move, you tell them to "rattle your hocks!"

Do you know the difference between a fox and a rabbit when they are running? The fox is running for his dinner, but the rabbit is running for his life! Sometimes, it's the incentive that makes all the difference.

I recall my Grandfather Benton describing a fellow he knew years ago that wasn't very big. He said that "He was so skinny, he had to stand twice to leave a shadow!" It could have been said that "He was as thin as tissue paper", or "He was as thin as a rail."

Country folks have their own way of expressing their thanks. Many times I've heard them say, "Much obliged." Another familiar expression is, "I 'preciate it", or just simply "preciate it!" (That's short for "appreciate!") I've heard my Dad say many times that he didn't mind helping someone if he knew it was appreciated.

Another quaint expression that I remember hearing when I was a youngster had to do with folks having lots of problems. One fellow who had a bunch of troubles was asked by another fellow to help him with his crisis. The answer to this request was quickly addressed with the statement, "I've got more problems now than I can say 'grace' over!" In other words, he already had enough problems of his own without taking on someone else's troubles.

During my early years on the farm it wasn't unusual for some folks to seek help to bring them good luck from "outside" sources. An example of this was the belief that carrying a rabbit's foot on their keychain or in their pocket would bring them good luck. Some folks wouldn't dare go anywhere without their rabbit's foot. If something unpleasant happened to them, you would probably hear someone say, "He's lost his rabbit's foot!" (It certainly wasn't "good luck" for the rabbit, was it?)

Another supposedly "good luck" item that was commonly sought in those by-gone days was a four-leaf clover. Finding a four-leaf clover was widely thought to bring good luck. I can remember searching diligently in our yard hoping to find one. Common sense and reasoning now compels me to realize that a rabbit's foot or a four-leaf clover really doesn't have anything to do with our fortune or misfortune. I guess folks were "grasping at straws" hoping to somehow improve their lot in life.

Sometimes when folks found themselves in a daily grind, and

there wasn't much prospect of improving their circumstances, it was said that they were "in a rut." One fellow described a rut as "a grave with both ends knocked out!" (Depressing, isn't it?)

A humorous tid-bit of "tom-foolery" has to do with someone arriving at the wrong conclusion concerning another person's actions. Sometimes folks would have the facts all wrong, and would proceed to spread the "facts" around, even though they were incorrect. When this happened, the one spreading the false gossip was said to be "barking up the wrong tree!" This saying comes from the habit of some hunting dogs, such as a 'coon dog, of following the scent trail of some animal other than a 'coon, until the scent trail led to a tree. The 'coon dog was supposed to follow the scent trail of only a 'coon, but some of the 'coon dogs would follow the trail of other animals, such as a 'possum. Thus, when the hunter came to the tree where the dog was barking at the "treed" animal, he expected to find a 'coon. If there was a 'possum up the tree, the dog was "barking up the wrong tree!'

Having spent the first 18 years of my life on a farm, my outlook on life was formed from a rural perspective. Since those days, I see the world through the filter of a farming background. For example, most of the fields on our farm that were used for crops were not squares or rectangles. That meant that on part of the field, around the edge, there would be rows that were shorter than those in the middle. Whenever there was work to be done in the crop fields, you always wanted to get to the shorter rows. Now, think about any task that you might undertake in life. An expression rural folks used to indicate that the hardest part of a chore was finished, and the job was almost over, was to say they were "down to the short rows!"

When someone was well off financially, and he was "enjoying the good life", he was said to be in "tall cotton!"

To find yourself in a crowded room with lots of folks, or driving on the highway and the road was "jammed" with traffic, "everybody and his brother" was there!

If you met someone that you hadn't seen in a long time, or someone appeared that wasn't dressed properly, you were sure to hear, "Look what the cat drug in", or "You're a sight for sore eyes!"

From time to time there would be something that happened that was out of the ordinary realm. Country folks have an expression that pretty much covers anything unusual. At such times they would say, "Boy, now that's a "humdinger!"

Country folks have certain expressions that address their "putting aside" money in a savings account at the local bank. This is referred to as "salting some money away", or " saving money for a rainy day." At hog-killing time on the farm, the hams and shoulders would be covered with salt and hung in the smokehouse in order to preserve them for later use. Preserving money was "salting it away!"

When searching for something and the likelihood of finding it is almost zero, it is said to be like "looking for a needle in a haystack!"

When in the presence of a lady, and her slip was showing below her dress, you could inform her of this by saying, "It's snowing down South!" A gentleman would never discuss her undergarments in "plain" language.

A country expression that was used to indicate that something was over and done with, was to say, "It's Katie bar the door!" And, if you was talking about the sum of everything someone owned, it was "the whole kit and kaboodle!"

If someone was going through life with no real sense of direction, he was said to be running around "like a chicken with it's head cut off!"

There's a good friend of our family whose name is Will. He is 21 years old and at the time that I'm writing this, is serving with our country's armed services in Iraq. He and my son, Kevin, who is scheduled to be commissioned as a Second Lieutenant in the U.S. Marine Corps in a few days, are "best buddies." Some time after my wife passed away, I was watching television one night and an advertisement about eHarmony.com came on. Eharmony.com is a couple's matching service. I decided to give it a try and I signed up. After receiving several possible "matches", I was shown the one of my present wife, Linda. It was a match "made in Heaven" and we fit together like a "hand in a glove!"

Anyway, Will, who is a very fine-looking, handsome young man, the sort of guy who isn't involved in "tom-foolery" or "bodacious ballyhoo," wasn't having a lot of luck in meeting someone romantically. He was so impressed with my good fortune in finding Linda that he decided to sign up with eHarmony.com and give it a try. At last report, he hadn't found anybody that "perked his interest". I feel sure that there is a young lady somewhere "out there" that will be just right for Will. The military service sort of interrupted his plans for now, but I'll bet it wont be long before he'll give it another try. I hope you find her, Will! Ahoy & Anchors Aweigh!

Chapter 10

Down on the Farm Proverbs

MONEY   TREE ?

F.G.W.
10

Listening to my Grandfather Benton (Mom's Dad) and other elderly family members, there seemed to be a steady stream of proverbs espoused for our general good. The rural humor is refreshing and indicates lessons learned the "hard way." Among these was this: "There never was a bird that flew so high that it didn't have to come down to earth sometime." Or, "What goes up must come down." Or, "What goes around comes around."

Then there's this jewel: "The grass is always greener on the other side of the fence."

I can still hear my parents telling me: "Money doesn't grow on trees, you know!" We were cautioned not to "take any wooden nickels." Say what?

One of my favorites is: "You can lead a horse to water, but you can't make him drink." "Better fifteen minutes early than one minute late" was one that was expressed often at home.

I especially like this one: "Reputation is who you think I am. Character is who I am!"

"Be sure to look a gift horse in the mouth" ranked right up there with "All that glitters is not gold." In other words, not everyone you meet is honest in his dealings!

"If it looks like a duck, walks like a duck, and quacks like a duck, it probably is a duck!" On the other hand, "You can't judge a book by its cover."

Ever have trouble getting everyone to bed on time? "A short night makes for a long day." Conversely, "A long night makes for a short day!" Wow, imagine that!

I've heard Mom express this one many times: "A watch pot never boils." How about: "A word once spoken can never be retrieved." "To err is human, but to forgive divine."

Then, this one: "Sticks and stones may break my bones, but words will never harm me." (Oh, yes they will!)

"If you lie with dogs, you're going to get fleas." Here's a zinger: "You can't take it with you!" Or, "I've never seen a U-Haul following a hearse to the cemetery." (Is there an object lesson here somewhere?)

I recall Mom saying: "It only takes one rotten apple to spoil the whole barrel." I wouldn't want to be that one that's rotten! Last, but not least: "an ounce of prevention is worth a pound of cure."

Growing up on the farm in the '40s and '50s was very different than it is today. Back then folks usually didn't lock their houses or their motor vehicles. Although there were a few "rotten apples" (criminals) among us, you seldom heard of anyone breaking into a house or a car.

It was very common for a farmer to have an understanding with his neighbor that if he needed a particular tool or a piece of farm machinery, he had permission to go get it, use it, and then return it to its proper place. Folks would treat the borrowed item just like it was their own, and would always be sure of its condition before returning it.

Another common practice back then was to swap out labor. Sometimes, farmers would gather at a particular farm and finish a job, such as baling the hay, housing the tobacco, etc. Then, they would go to another farmer's place and get his job done. It was a really neat way of cooperating among themselves to get the jobs done. One example of this cooperative spirit was a "barn raising." If a farmer was building a new barn, the men folks would gather at the building site, and erect the barn, usually in a matter of a couple or three days. The women folks would prepare meals on site so the men could eat quickly.

There was one piece of advice that I heard at least a "zillion" times as I was growing up that had to do with getting in a hurry to do something. Just as sure as the sun comes up in the East and sets in the West, you were sure to hear, "Keep your shirt on", or "Hold your horses!" Now, doesn't that make a lot of sense? "City slickers" missed a lot in not growing up on the farm.

Mom used to say that "Idle hands is the Devil's workshop." If that's the case, he was surely "out of business", because we were kept busy every day!

Today's families operate under a different agenda than when I was growing up. For example, when I was a youngster, the percentage of adult women that worked outside of the home was much smaller than it is today. Women were nurses, secretaries, teachers and beauticians as a general rule. When World War 2 began, women began working in factories doing what had previously been a man's job, because men were off fighting the war. A classic example of this was "Rosie, the riveter." After the war was over, women didn't necessarily want to return to being "just a housewife." Today, women make up a major portion of the work force. Consequently, children today grow up under a different set of circumstances. We seem to have lost the "close-knit" family circle of yesteryear!

When we were growing up, Dad used to talk about different groups of people, and how they related to each other. He seemed to believe that some folks just weren't aware of how people in other parts of the world lived. I've heard him express it like this: "Half the world has no idea of how the other half lives!" One thing that I observed about Dad was that he read the newspapers, listened to the news on the radio, and talked with other folks in front of the courthouse every Saturday in order to keep up with what was going on in the world around him. And, of course, he talked with people who came into his grocery store, especially in the evenings when other farmers would come by and sit and talk for hours about things they all had in common. He didn't believe that folks should "bury their heads in the sand", and therefore isolate themselves from other people. Be engaged!

Some folks just naturally seem to be unable to take control of their lives and how to plan their future. One problem they have is in being financially responsible. If they are able to earn some money, they have difficulty using it properly to their advantage. They are susceptible to any scheme that comes along that looks "too good to be true." There is a saying that country folks have for this: "A fool and his money are soon parted!"

From time to time you would hear someone gossiping about a person, and the one spreading the gossip would be guilty of the same thing he was telling. When this happened, he was said to be like the "pot calling the kettle black!"

Tenant farmers would grow crops on another farmer's land.. They were said to be growing crops "on the halves" or "on the shares."

Chapter 11

Sage Advice

CART IN FRONT OF HORSE?

F.G.W.
#12

In my formative years there was always people giving out advice. It seemed as if we were constantly bombarded with these sage pieces of wisdom.

"Don't count you chickens before the eggs hatch." (If I've heard that one once, I've heard it a bunch of times.)

"Look before you leap" precludes being hasty about something.

Operate on the side of caution! "If you play with fire, you're going to get burned." Or, "If you wallow in mud, you're going to get muddy." (Duh!)

Living on the farm produced some natural words of advice, such as: "Everybody's chickens come home to roost sooner or later!" "People who live in glass houses shouldn't throw stones."

How about: "Don't put the cart (or wagon) in front of the horse?" Now, wouldn't that be a silly sight? Or, "First things first!"

"If you want to get ahead in this world, do more than is expected of you" was one of my Dad's admonishments. This one really got my attention: "Don't get caught with your pants down!" Another version was: "Don't get caught with your hand in the cookie jar."

Sex education was simple and direct: "Keep your skirt down (girls), and your pants up (boys)." Girls were advised to "Keep your legs crossed at all times!" We didn't have to learn about the birds and the bees. We watched the cattle, the horses, the hogs, and the poultry, etc. Even a country boy could figure it out eventually!

"Don't get ahead of the hounds" is only understood by someone who has gone fox or 'coon (raccoon) hunting. When you went hunting, you would convey the hound dogs to a likely place and turn them loose. They would circle around until they came upon the scent of a fox or a 'coon and then follow it. The hunters would lag behind until the hounds had run the 'coon up a tree or the fox into a den in the ground. Then, the hunters could either bag the animal or let it go free if they didn't want to kill it. One thing you didn't want to do was chase after the hounds until they had done their job which was to "tree" or "den" the animal. Makes sense when you think about it.

A really great piece of advice is: "Better to keep your mouth shut and have people think you're a fool, than to open it and remove all doubt!"

One thing I remember from my tour of duty in the Navy as a radio operator was this one: "You were broadcasting when you should have been tuning in." (In other words, you were talking when you should have been listening!)

"Don't belly ache" meant don't complain!

"If it needs to be done, why not do it now?" Or, "Don't put off until tomorrow what needs to be done today." "Do the tough job first and get it behind you." "If it's worth doing, it's worth doing well!"

"Put your money where your mouth is." Or, "Either fish or cut bait!" In other words, if you're going to do it, do it! If you was "pussy-footing around" or "lolly-gagging," that meant you was wasting time.

"Little children should be seen, not heard" ranked up there with "Don't speak unless spoken to."

Dad would say, "You'll learn more by listening than by speaking." Also, "All the world's knowledge is in books. Go to the library and learn from them!" I remember when I would be reading and if I came across a word that I didn't know the meaning of or how to pronounce it, Dad would tell me to look it up in the dictionary and see how it was pronounced and learn the definition(s) of it. Good advice!

Dad was what I like to call an "aw, shucks philosopher!" He had an eighth grade education, but he was one of the most intelligent men I have ever met. He could do most anything with his hands, and he had plenty of common sense.

Dad was firm, but fair, and Mom was tender and long-suffering. They complimented each other when it came to raising us ten children. Can you imagine trying to raise ten children in today's society?

If a youngster was beginning to form some bad habit, such as smoking or using 'foul' language, usually the parents of older siblings would attempt to stop him from doing so. An expression that addressed this situation was to say: "I'm going to nip this in the bud!" Most everyone knows that in the spring time all trees and flowers produce new buds that bring forth flowers or fruit. Thus, if you "nip" or break off the bud, there will not be any flower or fruit brought to maturity. To stop a bad habit from forming, you "nip it in the bud!"

Another interesting piece of advice that country folks sometimes give has to do with when someone is trying to achieve something and the likelihood of it being successful is hopeless. As "sure as shootin'", you were bound to hear, "You're on a wild goose chase!" I don't know if you've ever tried to catch a wild goose or not, but it is futile. If you was to try a hundred times to catch a wild goose, using nothing but your hands, the score after the hundredth time would be: goose = 100, human = 0. Nuf said!

We used to have a dog at home and one of his favorite things to do was to chase after his own tail. Try as he might, he could never catch it! Could it be said that the dog was on a "wild goose chase?" It must have been frustrating for him to be so close to his tail and never quite able to reach it! Talk about an exercise in futility. Holy mackerel!

When I was a youngster growing up on the farm, it was considered quite normal to be a "farm boy." In those days, about half of the population lived in rural America. When the Industrial Revolution came along, and factories became plentiful, more and more farm folks moved into the cities. The number of farms across America began to diminish and a way of life in this country began to change. Today, only about five percent of our population is directly involved in farming. The small farms were either bought up by farming conglomerates, or the farm land was turned into suburban communities.

I can remember seeing my Dad following behind a turning plow that was pulled by two horses as he got the soil ready for a crop. Today, a huge tractor pulls a gang-plow that does in one hour, or less, what it took my Dad an entire day to do. I can remember how tired he was at the end of the day after plowing. Now, farm machinery costing thousands of dollars, sometimes hundreds of thousands, are required to do the work. I can't help but wonder what Dad would say if he could see how farming is done today.

Chapter 12

Code of Ethics

TIPPING HIS HAT TO A LADY

F. G. W.
11

D own on the farm as I was growing up I was exposed to a code of ethics that was to be my guide to influence my behavior.

For example, I was admonished to always tell the truth. My Dad told me that if I always told the truth, I wouldn't have to ever "look back over my shoulder." He also said that the "truth was the truth, no matter where you found it." To speak of someone's honesty in a meaningful way was to say, "He's as honest as the day is long." Another way of putting forth this same truth was to say, "He'd rather cut his arm off than to tell a lie." Telling a lie was to tell a "big'un" or a "whopper." If someone habitually lied, it was said that "He wouldn't know the truth if he heard it!" If a story didn't ring true, it "didn't add up." My Dad would say: "If a man lies to you, he'll also steal from you," or "If a man steals from you, he will also lie to you." I recall my Dad telling us: "Remember, your word is your bond."

One thing I found fascinating during my youth was to hear how people described another person that was rather blunt. You could seemingly say anything about someone else as long as you concluded the statement with, "Bless his/her heart!" If some lady was not especially attractive, she might be described as "plain as an old cow, bless her heart", or a man might be described as "ugly as an ape, bless his heart!"

When given a choice of things to do, you might hear a response like, "If I had my druthers, I'd do such and such." This was another way of saying what your preference was. "If I had my druthers" was another way of saying, "This is what I'd rather do."

Among the strict up-bringing lessons we were taught as youngsters were these nuggets: a gentleman opened doors for a lady; men tipped their hats to a lady; men removed their hats upon entering a residence; a man would rise and offer his seat to a lady if there were no empty seats; men walked on the outside of the sidewalk nearest to the traffic for her safety. And you never passed gas in the presence of a lady or in church. Chivalry isn't dead these days, it's just feeling poorly!

Included in our code of ethics was the admonishment to never speak vulgar or dirty language in a lady's presence. If we were caught doing this by our parents, we were told to "Go wash your mouth out with lye soap!" Yuk! Can you imagine that?

One piece of advice that Mom often shared with us at home was in reference to discussions about other people. If any of us began saying anything negative about some other person, Mom was sure to tell us, "If you can't say something good about someone, don't say anything at all!" I can honestly say that in all of my lifetime that Mom was alive, I never heard her say anything negative about someone else. WOW! She used to say "There is some good in everybody."

There's an expression that originated out West. It had to do with the dependability of an individual when the "going got tough." If you had a friend that you could always rely on to be there for you, he was said to be someone "to ride the river with." Picture in your mind rafting down a white-water stream. In order to successfully navigate this body of water, it would be necessary for everyone to do his part. If your friend did his part every time, he was someone "to ride the river with." And, speaking of rivers, another "zinger" was one that had to do with someone betraying you that you thought you could count on. When this happened, it was said that you was "sold down the river!"

When you was swapping or trading with someone, and you got the worst of the deal, you was said to have gotten "the short end of the stick!" This would also apply if you was treated unfairly and didn't get equal treatment as others.

There were some subjects that folks did not discuss when making conversation. Among them were things like religion, politics, private and personal behavior. For example, you would not try to tell someone that his religious belief (or lack thereof) was all wrong and then proceed to try to convince him that your belief was the correct one. At times folks, especially men, would talk about an upcoming political election and maybe express their preference for a particular candidate. But, you would never tell someone that the candidate that he favored was a poor choice. Also, you never discussed someone else's wife or girl friend of sister, etc. And, you never pried or got nosy about another's personal finances. As a youngster I was cautioned to never ask an adult lady her age. And, all adults were addressed as "Mr., Mrs., or Miss." You never addressed an adult by their first name. All of these subjects were considered "ill mannered."

Can you remember when wearing green and blue together was considered poor taste? If you wore stripes and plaids together, you was 'uncouth!' You never wore white before Easter nor after Labor Day. Whatever happened to those practices?

When I would tell my Mom that I loved her, she often replied, "Don't tell me you love me. Show me." Dad used to admonish us about our behavior when we were leaving home by telling us, "I'd rather be proud of you than ashamed." I remember him telling me on one occasion that his Mom and Dad had given him a good name, and he always tried to make them proud of him. My parents have been dead for several years now, and I still am influenced every day by them. I would never do or say anything that would bring dishonor to them.

When leaving the house we were admonished to "Remember whose child you are." Another zinger was: "You're known by the company you keep."

Mom lacked one week living to be 85 years old when she passed away. Think about raising ten children and all that that implies. Think about all the cloth diapers that she had to wash and bleach until the children were 'potty trained!' (This was before the days of disposable diapers.) Think about all the clothes she washed and the meals she prepared, all the clothing she made on the sewing machine at home, doing all the housework, and all the other things she accomplished during her tenure on earth. I salute you, Mom!

Dad lived 82 years and three months, and he was just as impressive. He worked hard all of his life and provided the family with all the necessities of life. He worked in the oil fields, worked in a rock quarry during the Depression, lost his savings when the bank failed, and farmed for a great number of years, as well as running a "jot'em down" grocery. No one ever questioned his integrity. I salute you, Dad!

CPSIA information can be obtained
at www.ICGtesting.com
Printed in the USA
BVHW04s0157150618
519079BV00003B/39/P